Puppies

Your guide to
successful ownership

Angela White

The above photograph by John Treu. Front cover photograph by Sue Domun.

Puppies

contents

acknowledgements

As always in our daily lives and in our place of work there are many people warranting mention and thanks for their support, interest, help and encouragement. In the preparation of this book there have been some people without whom it would have been very difficult to complete the task.

Gail Thornton (VN), Animal Care Course Manager and lecturer at Bishop Burton College, for helping to get the message of sound behavioural knowledge and motivational training over to the students and masses, for technical guidance and advice on health and first aid, and also for allowing me unlimited access to her own puppies to extend my catalogue of puppy assessments, and to help with some of the photographs in this book.

Lynette Nicholson (City & Guilds Grooming), lecturer at Bishop Burton College, for her expert guidance and for sharing her wealth of knowledge for the grooming section.

Belinda Pattrick, for proof-reading and offering constructive criticism, as well as allowing me to relate to, and spend hours observing the behaviour of her own animals, recording data and sequential character potential assessments on her pups. Also, her husband, Trevor Pattrick, for being ever-supportive and giving unconditional help and friendship when it was needed most in our joint and individual ventures.

Tom Newbould for casting his expert eye over the text to eradicate 'Angie's Bloomers'!

The models, both human and canine, who gave up their time to pose for photographs in the book, and the many readers of Smart Dogs and Obedience Competitor who allowed their own photographs to be included. My husband, Mike, contributed the rest of the photographs – many thanks.

And finally ... to my immediate family: husband Mike, son Daniel and my Mum who as always, while I hide away in my writer's solitude, give encouragement, support and keep me topped up with hot drinks, food and lots of love.

dedication

To all of you who take time out to read this book in order to give your dog a stress-free, full and enjoyable life. The dog has few choices, you have many – I hope this book will help you to make the right choices for your dog.

introduction

Over the years the ideas and techniques of training dogs have changed and been modified to help us to have better-behaved dogs, and animals that are more suited to living in our domestic environments.

In general, the aim is still the same, that is, to have an animal which fits into the family structure, is well behaved at home as well as in public, perhaps fulfils certain tasks and, above all, is a pleasure to own.

In order to fulfil this ambition we must know and understand the structure of what we are trying to achieve.

To understand that the dog thinks in a different way from humans is an essential part of our comprehension of the dog. To

understand the way in which it learns, what motivates it, and what induces strong responses such as fear, anxiety, excitement, aggression, dominance, placidity and boredom is an important factor in how we deal with our pets.

To keep full control of your pet means that you must always be aware and fully alert to its reactions, instincts, responses and needs. A dog will never be a human; it will never think like a human, no matter how much training you do, and no matter how much you feel that it has taken on human characteristics. You will never be able fully to predict its behaviour in changing circumstances. Even when your pet is fully trained, there will be times when its behaviour will surprise you, and at these times you must remember that it is a dog – an animal with animal responses. You must always expect the unexpected.

This book will help you to understand the needs, both physical and mental, of your puppy, and to prevent errors of judgement that will cause problems for you and your pet. The main criterion is to promote enjoyment for you, your family, those around you and, of course, the pup, and to give you the ability to control and train your pet to a level that you can be both comfortable with and proud of.

There are minor repetitions throughout the book, because it is intended to be used as a reference, and therefore each chapter should make sense even when referred to in isolation. Of course, to get the best benefit from the book you should read it in its entirety.

In most instances the dog or puppy is referred to as 'it', but the owners, handlers and trainers are generally called 'he'. This is for ease of reading only and, of course, unless referred to as specifically male, the masculine refers to both sexes and is not in any way intended to show a preference or bias to males.

The dog has control over few choices that affect its destiny – you have many. You control the future of your pet – don't let it down!

West Highland White, owned by M Johnston
Photograph by Robert Smith

understanding
puppies

Right from the start, even before you attempt to bring up any animals, including children, it helps to understand as much as possible about them. All animals have certain needs and, if these are fulfilled in a way that is both satisfying and meaningful, then you are well on the way to having a well-controlled pet.

The dog is a pack animal and so needs to feel part of a pack. It is important, particularly in domestic situations, that the pup understands where its position is within that pack, and that all the other pack members (people) maintain a higher position in the hierarchy than it does.

Because we are, in theory, more intelligent than our friend the dog, we have to make sure the pup understands all of this. This means not allowing the pup to make decisions or control situations for itself until it understands the guidelines of the household. It needs to feel safe, and it needs to know who is in control. For the pup, it is rather like learning the rules of a complicated game, except that it is not aware it has to learn them! It therefore takes quite a while for the pup to be sure of all the implications and idiosyncrasies. We have learned that protocol and conforming play a part in survival and the pup needs to learn this as well.

The pup's mind does not work in the same way as ours; it does not think backwards and forwards, nor solve problems with lateral or conscious thinking. Instead, it reacts to situations as they happen by using what it has learned will work, with an instinctive reaction, by trial and error, or a combination of the three.

Like you, your pup can be affected by hormones and other bodily changes and conditions. For instance, ill health, pain and puberty all influence its reactions, just as they do ours.

Like all animals, the dog is inclined to keep away from things that are unpleasant, boring, mundane, monotonous, unrewarding, unnatural or frightening. It will strive for things that bring it pleasure and enjoyment, as well as things that are needed for its survival, both of an immediate nature and to ensure that its own genes influence its species.

The pup's mental state will affect its whole well-being, just as our minds can affect our own behaviour and physical condition.

It is important to realise the needs of the pup's bodily functions as well as its mind. It needs to go to the toilet more often than an adult dog. It needs to eliminate from its system unwanted fluid and solids many times in a day: when it has eaten, when it wakes from sleep, when it gets excited, even when it is afraid. It needs to eat little and often to enable it to digest the amount of calories it needs. It needs lots of rest, as well as constructive play to help it to learn.

This book will help you to understand your puppy at the different stages of its development, and how to take into account the various ways in which evolution and genetics have influenced this carnivorous predator that we have taken into our homes as a pet.

We also examine the role that you and your family will play in the choice, care, attitude towards, and training of the pup, and how this too will have an effect on your pup's behaviour and health.

understanding puppies

There is much more to the bringing up of a healthy, well-controlled pup than first meets the eye. The more you learn, the easier it will become, and the more competent and comfortable you will feel towards the training and care of your pup.

Bedlington Terriers photographed by Gerald Coley.

how to choose
a puppy

Having a new puppy is an event that affects the whole family and, therefore, the whole family should be consulted before a decision is made. The decision affects each member of the family in a different way and, if anyone is not happy, or does not give sufficient thought to how they will be affected, then the end result could be disastrous.

Some members of the family may not be able to make relevant contributions to the discussion. Young children and even some adults cannot make realistic practical comments, because they may be ruled by emotion or what might be termed 'cuddle syndrome'; that is, the sight or thought of a cuddly puppy means that the heart rules the head. Others may not be aware of the way in which a puppy will affect them, particularly if they are not accustomed to dogs. If the last family pet was an old dog, set in its ways, that fitted the family with the comfort of the proverbial 'old shoe', it is hard to imagine the difference that a new puppy will make – even one of the same breed. Many people fall into the trap of expecting the new pup to be the same as 'old Fido' used to be. Even if 'old Fido' was the same breed, do not expect your 'Fido Mark Two' to react in the same way. All dogs are different, even if they come from the same breed lines. Don't blame the puppy if it doesn't come up to your expectations.

Some people have a false idea regarding a dog's capabilities, and the media, although extremely entertaining, has played its part in making trained animals, such as Lassie and Beethoven to name but two, appear to have very believable human-like or even super-human powers.

Have you the space to keep a large or active dog, such as this German Shepherd Dog?

how to choose a puppy

The whole family needs to realise that life will not be the same when the new puppy arrives and that, as it develops, things may get worse before they get better! The fact that you are reading this book means that you are going to make sure that the puppy does not get out of control, and learns the 'house rules' very quickly. Nevertheless, you can be sure that the wolf in cute puppy clothing will make itself at home in a big way!

the time factor

How much time do you have available to deal with this puppy? If you have a busy working life, then you must consider the consequences of leaving the pup for long periods of time. You may need a dog sitter to care for the dog when you are not able to give it your full attention. Perhaps you will need an outside area with a kennel and enclosure (see chapter 8).

Perhaps it is not ideal for you to have a pup at all if your time is so limited that you cannot give it sufficient attention to keep it occupied, healthy and happy. I am

The Bichon Frisé does not moult – but consider the amount of grooming it will need.

not suggesting that just because you have a full-time job you should not have a pup, but you must be aware of its needs and make the necessary arrangements for its well-being. Many full-time workers make excellent homes for puppies, but these are the type of people who take holiday from work initially to settle the pup into its new environment, and to get it into a routine so that it knows where it stands. They also make all necessary arrangements for the pup to be taken care of by someone else who is 'dog wise' and keen to be involved whilst they are out.

Some people are lucky enough to be able to have the dog with them while they work, but this means that breaks and spare time must be spent attending to the demands of the bundle of mischief, and not chatting about TV programmes or the latest fashions. A crate (see chapters 7 and 8), will be a wise investment for those who must stick to a timetable. The pup will soon adjust to your routine, as long as the periods between it getting attention are not too long, and the attention then given is of good quality.

As the pup matures, things get a little less demanding, but then other problems occur if the pup is left to its own devices with insufficient stimulus.

In general, a busy working home is not an ideal environment for a puppy, but understanding the needs of the pup more fully will help you to make your own decision, and to weigh up the pros and cons with both the dog and the family's well-being in mind.

Choose a pup that will fit in with your life style. Photograph by J. Pryor

Rare breeds like this Leonberger make heads turn.

activity level

If your family enjoys an out-of-doors and active lifestyle, then an energetic type of breed often fits in well. There are many breeds that meet this criterion, but you should consider other factors of the dog's make up before you choose one of the more obviously active breeds such as the Border Collie. I have nothing against the Border Collie as a breed – at the time of writing I have three of my own – but they do come with their own set of idiosyncrasies, as do many breeds, and these factors must be considered before the family makes its final decision.

If, on the other hand, the family prefers a more sedentary existence, then choose a breed that will be happy with this life. All dogs need a certain amount of exercise, as do humans, and perhaps many of us could do with a little more! But buying a Border Collie in the hope that it will stimulate the family into activity may result in disaster.

why do you want your pup?

The reasons why you and your family want a new puppy and your expectations should be considered very carefully. If everyone is expecting something different from the dog, the poor animal could end up very confused! For instance, if Mum wants a house dog, a protector and a companion, she may be looking for different qualities than the children, who want a happy-go-lucky fun dog to join in their games. Then there's Dad, who may want a dog he can take down to the pub, or to find and collect his missing golf balls! There are many breeds able and happy to do all of this, but of course there are breeds that just would not fit the bill.

You may be of the opinion that if you buy a 'good' dog or bitch you may be able to make some money from breeding – do not be so sure. There are many factors that must

how to choose a puppy

be taken into consideration before breeding, and there are absolutely no guarantees of you ever making any money at all. In fact, more often than not, you will end up spending more than you make; a pup is definitely not a 'get rich quick' machine.

The family may all agree on choosing from a certain selection – perhaps the larger breeds appeal to you all – but do you all have the same image of the attitude and characteristics of that dog? Is Mum imagining a large, graceful, relatively quiet dog, whilst the children visualise it playing football with them for hours on end? Oh, I forgot Dad again, perhaps he had ideas of going out shooting with his gundog!

There is another factor to consider, and that is how you will feel in public with your breed. Some people would not feel comfortable walking a Maltese, whilst others would not be happy with a Bulldog. You may think that the man of the house is being stupid if he refuses to take out your lapdog, but consider your pet – will it make a difference to the dog if

Remember how big the Great Dane pup will grow!

some of its family refuse to be seen out with it? On the other hand, some of the family may be ecstatic over the thought of having a Rottweiler, but do all the members feel that they have the physical and mental capabilities to cope with a strong dog that could weigh as much as 50–60kg (8–10 stone) when fully grown?

People often sneer when a dog is bought to suit a macho image but, more often than not, dogs *are* bought for their looks, and other factors are given much lesser importance. It is imperative that you try not to be too extreme for the good of the dog and, indeed, the family. You should go for the breed that you *all* feel comfortable with, considering looks, physique and personality. We all have differing views when it comes to the concept of beauty on the outside but, if you cannot live with what comes from within, then the whole thing will collapse around you.

chapter two

choosing the right breed

Unless you have clear view of what you want from your dog, choosing the right breed for you can be an interesting yet difficult prelude to the new arrival.

There are tendencies within types: for instance, small breeds generally live longer than large breeds. Some breeds have more genetic disorders or life-threatening complaints than others. Some breeds have a greater tendency towards being dominant. Some breeds are more likely to be highly active. Some breeds settle to a quiet existence. Some breeds require much mental or physical control (or both). Some breeds are more likely to tolerate other animals. Some breeds are easy to motivate. Some breeds suffer from media hype. And so on.

There is much to be taken into account when embarking on a new venture of this sort, and it all boils down to fitting a dog into your own personal preferences and situation. Making the right choice will set you on the road to a great adventure with your dog – make the wrong choice and you could end up parting with the animal that you thought would be with you for many years.

If you are undecided or cannot agree on a breed, sit down with the family and make out a chart or list of all of your hopes and expectations. The chart should be your own variation on the one on page 15. Set out your likes and dislikes, and the things that you consider a problem and those that you do not. List your aspirations and dreams of what the dog might give you and what, in turn, you can give to the dog.

Puppies at an RSPCA Rescue Centre.   Photograph by Miss T B Chadwick

how to choose *a puppy*

So go ahead, add your own particular ideas to the chart.

	Mum	Dad	Son	Daughter	Sitter	Others
Likes Active/busy Exercising Intelligent Guarding Large Small Medium Long coat Short coat Terriers Grooming Bull breeds Rare breeds						
Dislikes Yapping Shedding Guarding Short coats Terriers Grooming Lapdogs Squashy faces! Active Sheep chasers Expense						
Wants Trainability Guard Lapdog No hairs Long walks Short walks Live out Live in Friendly Calm Lively						
Problems Barking Hairs Guarding Dominance Space Slobbering Energy Kennelling Time Money Neighbours Travel Other pets						

Do not be influenced by cute pictures.
Photograph courtesy of Sheila Hocken

Once you have come up with all the things you like and dislike, fill in the chart by ticking the relevant boxes. Then look at the chart and work out what dog you would like by comparing your answers with breeds in general or specific breed books or encyclopedias of dog breeds. The registered Kennel or Breed Club Standard for the breed will give you an idea of what breeders are striving towards, in both temperament and looks.

Be very careful when referring to books with league tables showing character traits. These can be of value, but it is best to read a few to get a cross-section of opinions. Often these charts reflect the author's experience with a breed and not a more general attitude. If you are living in the United Kingdom and the author is, say, Australian, there may be many traits in breed lines that are not seen in your country but are common in Australia. Even in the same country, breed lines differ tremendously, so never take the written word as a blueprint of what you will get.

Once you have rendered your decisions down to one or two breeds, read as much as you can on those breeds, track down some people who have those breeds and ask questions relating to all aspects of their dogs' lives, behaviour and well-being. For instance, how often is the dog ill, are the illnesses hereditary, does the dog have any behavioural problems, what is it like to live with? Compare the answers with what you already know of the breed, apply it to your personal situation, and add a large helping of common sense.

Do not assume that all behavioural problems are down to the breed or breed line; most problems of this type are caused by incorrect handling and few dogs are so laid back that they do not take advantage, given the opportunity. Certain breeds, and breed lines within breeds, have potentials and tendencies in their character which, if not carefully and correctly handled, may create problems for you. Others will carry the potential for physical defects, some of these defects being more of a problem than others. So think carefully before making sweeping or impulsive judgements.

how to choose *a puppy*

crossbreeds and mongrels

Crossbreed is the general term addressed to dogs when the parentage is known: for example, a cross between a Border Collie and a German Shepherd would be termed a crossbreed. The term 'crossbreed' would also be used to describe the progeny of a mating between one of these resultant puppies to another known cross. Basically, as long as the crosses are known then the dog is termed a crossbreed.

The term 'mongrel' is more generally used when the crosses or mixtures are not specifically known. Another affectionate term commonly used for this is 'Heinz 57', implying that there might be as many as, if not more than, 57 varieties of dog in the ancestry.

There are many benefits in choosing a non-pedigree dog as a pet, and there are always plenty to choose from. There are various sources to go to.

There are usually even more adult mongrels in rescue centres than puppies, and generally they cost far less than a pedigree dog. Gone are the days, however, when all rescue centres simply gave away the dogs. Many now ask a set price for the animals, or for a reasonable donation. This helps to maintain the standards of the rescue home, and also prevents animals being taken on a whim without proper consideration of the financial side of keeping a pet. If there is no set fee, you may be asked for a donation that will cover the costs of inoculations, worming and other veterinary treatment.

Some forward-thinking and compassionate rescue societies operate a variety of schemes to help you make the right choice for you and the dog. For instance, if you decide to take an older animal rather than a young dog or puppy, some societies help with veterinary fees, and holiday boarding if necessary. This provides the dog with a better lifestyle which, after all, is what the rescue home is all about. The society may also help with the cost of neutering. It is always worth seeing a few homes before making your decision. You will probably have to answer many questions about what you can offer the dog, and also may receive a home visit from one of the helpers who will assess whether you are in a position to offer a good home. The society will also offer advice on how best to help your new family member fit in.

Of course, rescue centres are not the only places where you can obtain your cross or mongrel puppy. Many people will mate a pure bred dog with another pure bred or known cross with the

Do not expect to get a pup for free from a rescue centre. Donations are always welcomed.

purpose of producing certain characteristics. Then, of course, there is the accidental mating: a bitch gets out of the garden, or a visiting dog gets in, or one of the bitch owner's own dogs finds his way to the on-heat bitch. Dogs can be very resourceful when driven by the urge to reproduce! These matings often produce wonderful progeny, which in caring and knowledgeable hands can end up as superb dogs.

At the other end of the scale are the street and country dogs who are allowed out to reproduce at will, resulting in puppies of very mixed and usually uncertain ancestry. The puppy you get may be one from a succession of litters from the same tired old bitch who no sooner gets over one litter than she finds herself producing another. This is bound to lead to inferior puppies, both mentally and physically. The danger of purchasing or obtaining a puppy from this background is that it may not have had a very good upbringing either nutritionally or behaviourally, so it may have intrinsic problems that are difficult for you to overcome. Having said that, many turn out well and make excellent pets.

Crossing breeds can often eliminate or lessen the incidence of hereditary diseases and, in general, crossbreeds and mongrels have fewer health problems than pedigree dogs, although this is by no means the situation for all mongrels. Statistically, vets do not see as many mongrels as pure breeds, but this could be due in part to the fact that the owners of pure bred dogs are more aware of possible problems within the breed and so seek advice more readily, or that possibly they are more affluent. If you have paid a lot of money for a dog, you are more likely to protect your investment by having it insured, and/or making regular visits to the vet. The person on a lower income may choose to treat simple ailments at home.

It is difficult to know how your mongrel puppy will turn out. It is a little easier to predict the future outcome with known crosses. Two of the best dogs I ever owned were a crossbreed and a mongrel. The crossbreed, Taffy, was a first cross German Shepherd/Border Collie. He grew to be larger than the Collie but smaller than a GSD, and sandy-gold in colour. He displayed the best of both breeds as he matured, and for my purposes (which at that time was competing in Obedience) he was a superb dog. He recently passed away at the grand old age of sixteen and a half, and had only visited the vet once in his life other than for inoculations and neutering.

The mongrel, Guacha, was of medium size, and displayed very similar behaviour and had the abundance of coat of the Shetland Sheepdog (Sheltie), although she was considerably larger than the average Sheltie. When she met them she always enjoyed their company, and would actively seek them out at shows. I selected her from a litter that had been dumped when the pups were about five or six weeks old, and she was described by the RSPCA home as a cross Collie/German Shepherd that would grow very large. As she developed she displayed no behavioural characteristics of the GSD and very few of the Collie, and remained quite a lot smaller, although broader and more solidly-boned, than the average Border Collie – so who knows! At the age of 12, Guacha developed heart problems which was the first time she had to visit the vet. A couple of months later as we were considering ending her suffering she simply laid down in my office and never woke up.

rare breeds

There are benefits and drawbacks in choosing a rare breed. Undoubtedly, if you choose the sort of breed that people will stop and look at, you will make many new friends, as perfect strangers will ask you about your dog. It is imperative to work on your rare breed's temperament, not because it will have more problems than others, but because without doubt you will be expected to show it off more than the average Golden Retriever or Jack Russell.

When you take on a rare breed you are likely to be one of relatively few people who know the breed, and no doubt the other breeders and owners alike will be still finding out idiosyncrasies about temperament, ability, potential, health, and so on. This is the case even when the breed may be popular in other countries, as language barriers cause problems in technical details, and concepts, interpretations and expectations may differ with background and culture. Coupled with this is the fact that many breeders from this country and abroad do not have the ability, opportunity and sometimes, unfortunately, the integrity, to identify and point out all the problems. On top of all this, there is normally a small genetic pool (that is, many of the dogs are closely related), and if you are not careful you have a recipe for disaster.

Holly is a Pyrenean Sheepdog – a rare breed in the United Kingdom.

If you are new to a breed it is difficult to get to know all the possible genetic pitfalls, and usually you have to rely on a small number of breeders to give you the information that you require. Suffice to say that you must do your homework and find out as much as you can from as many sources as possible before making your choice.

There is a joy in seeing a breed progress and exploring the capabilities for yourself, to accomplish things as yet not achieved by others in the breed, and to promote and show off your masterpiece. However, you must be prepared for and accept that things may, and probably will, go wrong and it is advisable to learn from the mistakes made in other breeds, and by other breeders. There are always problems dealing with the unknown!

Rare breeds also often suffer from 'get-rich-quick' merchants who seek an opportunity to make high profits from dog breeding. This happens most particularly within the breeds that are more stunning, more unusual, produce large litters or are rapidly increasing in popularity, but even the less popular are not immune. Beware of the breeder who has been in and out of many different breeds which initially were high priced and then became cheaper. I must point out that not all breeders fall into the category of being unscrupulous and/or mercenary. Some genuinely enjoy the challenge of establishing a breed, and are very knowledgeable because of their past experiences. The breed may lose its appeal for them when it becomes popular and so they look around for something else. Even if the motivation is financial, it does not necessarily follow that they have made a bad job of it. It makes sense to produce excellent stock and get the best results in order to secure a prosperous business with a good reputation for the future. All I advise you to do is to ask questions and be careful where you choose.

Most rare breeds have their own breed club, and its secretary should be able to give you information on the history of the breed, its origins and its progress as far as your own country is concerned.

If you are sufficiently interested to promote the breed or to create your own breeding line, then you should be extra careful which bloodlines you choose. As with all breeds, you must take into account the possibilities of hereditary problems. Rare breeds tend to have a smaller gene pool, so that their problems are often highlighted and difficult to avoid.

getting two puppies

One last point: do not be tempted to have two puppies of about the same age, even if they are from the same litter. Although dogs are pack animals and prefer to have company, getting two of a similar age will give you all sorts of problems.

Bringing up a single puppy is an art, and is very time consuming. Trying to devote your care to two will mean splitting your available time in half, and neither pup will get the individual attention it needs. Puppies brought up together will bond together, and this means that *you* will not get the close relationship that you need to train and control the dogs correctly. You may intend to split them up, or have separate members of the family attend to them individually, but you will find that this will not happen because it is so much easier to allow the dogs to be together. You will try to treat them equally, but in practice this confuses the pack structure. As the puppies grow up, you will have to deal with hierarchy problems, especially if they are of the same sex, and sometimes this leads to quite severe battles.

If you have a brother and sister, the male probably will be sufficiently mature sexually to mate with the bitch as soon as she comes into her first season (oestrous cycle). Incest has no relevance to the canine mind, nor does the fact that the puppies' owner considers them too immature. Therefore you will need to make arrangements to separate them at this time. This will prove difficult and stressful, because neither pup will have learnt to be alone.

Any problems such as chewing, housetraining or barking, will be doubled because the pups will follow each other.

how to choose *a puppy*

If you really want two dogs, get one now, and then another at least a year later. This will give the first pup time to develop both mentally and physically.

So there are many factors to be taken into consideration before making your final decision and it is imperative that everyone whose lives will be affected should have a say in all the decisions.

Wait until your dog is older before introducing a new pup.
Photo of Bulldog and pup by Mr and Mrs Fairey

the *breeder*

where to look

How to find the right breeder depends upon the type of dog you are looking for, and requires your best detective work. The easiest way is to ask at dog clubs, go to relevant shows and then observe. Find a dog that you like and then ask the owner about its background, temperament, character and breeding. This gives you the chance to spend more time getting to know the individual dog and to assess its character in more informal circumstances. Most dog owners love to talk about their dog and, unless they are about to go into the ring, will gladly give you time, so don't be shy.

Dog magazines and papers often carry names of breeders and sometimes litters which are available. Also among the useful addresses at the back of this book there are companies and organisations that carry lists of breeders and sometimes lists of available litters.

stud dogs

In your search to find a good breeder, do not forget that the stud dog plays a big part in your pup's eventual character. If you find a good male dog that you really like, ask the owner if and when the dog will be used at stud, or ask for the name of the breeder who bred this dog. Often we focus on the idea of having a pup out of a dog that we really like, when in fact there is a better chance of getting something more like that particular dog by going back to its breeder and looking at the parents.

what to expect from the breeder

Breeders vary in their knowledge and ability, as well as their scruples. There is a great deal that can go wrong and, conversely, there is a great deal that the breeder can do right in order to give the puppies the best start possible. It has to be said that most problems are caused by ignorance; few breeders are uncaring enough to cause problems deliberately or through negligence. Anyone can breed a litter (there is no legislation to prevent this as yet), so there is bound to be a huge variation in standards. It is extremely difficult for the inexperienced, prospective puppy purchaser to identity the good from the mediocre.

Finding a licensed breeder will not automatically serve to safeguard the well-being of the puppies, although to maintain the licence the breeder must meet certain standards. At the end of the day, it is the individual care given to the pups that makes the difference, and this can be given equally well by unlicensed breeders. In fact, sometimes the attention lavished by the 'occasional' breeder outweighs the attention given by the breeder who has many animals to care for.

It is a fact that dogs mature better, are more balanced, have bigger brains, and are better able to deal with life when given individual attention for at least 40 minutes a day. This is difficult enough to achieve for the breeder with one large litter, but almost impossible for the breeder who has many other dogs to care for.

the breeder

Not all breeders are good sales people and if you ring and only ask the price of a puppy this may be all the information you are given. Ask questions about bloodlines, character, temperament, screening for hereditary disorders, nutrition, Kennel Club registration, parents' background, whether both parents can be seen, whether there are any puppies from previous litters that can be seen, and so on. Even if you are not sure what you are talking about, the more you ask, the more you will learn.

On the other hand, some breeders will 'blind you with science', and you may end up completely confused by the amount of information given. Do not be afraid to ask the breeder to explain or go over things again, as he will be happy to spend time with you if he cares about the breed and his puppies. The more you ask, the more you will learn and the more you will be able to weed out the facts from the exaggerations and omissions. It is always worth speaking to a selection of breeders if you are not *au fait* with the breed and its lines, as then you have more chance to understand and, therefore, avoid problems.

Puppies born in kennels at the National Canine Defence League Shelter, Darlington, getting love and attention.

Naturally, every breeder is a little biased in favour of his own dogs and related lines, as the object for most of them is to breed the type that they most like themselves, or that will win at shows. Therefore, take human nature into account when making your choices.

the breeder's responsibilities

Just as when any other item is sold, it is the seller's responsibility to make sure that the product is in good working order. However, it is impossible for the breeder to be sure how the pup will turn out and it would be foolhardy of him to make any promises. It is very much a case of 'you pay your money and you take your chance'.

The breeder should point out any potential hereditary problems, and tell you what he has screened for and, indeed, what you must screen for should you wish to breed from the dog in the future. If there are any specific hereditary problems, he should be able to explain to you the precautions he has taken in selecting the match between parents for this particular litter, and what he has tried to achieve by so doing.

If he has taken time to study the pups or has had puppy assessments done, he can tell you about the various characteristics and potentials that the pup has displayed in the first few weeks of life. He can also explain about any individual traits within his breed and his particular bloodlines, but after that it is up to the new owner to bring out the best in the pup.

The breeder should also supply a comprehensive diet guide, and information on inoculations, veterinary treatment and/or worming that has already been carried out, and when the next is due. Other added extras offered by breeders may include tattooing, books, leads, collars and other equipment, but this is not to be expected.

insurance

Many breeders sell the puppy with insurance to cover the first few weeks. After this, it is up to you, the purchaser, to carry on with the insurance if you feel you would like the benefit of this added peace of mind. The breeder will give you details of how to continue with the same company should you wish to, but you should shop around for insurance that suits your needs before making a decision, because there are many companies offering various schemes.

breeder's contract

It is not unusual nowadays for the breeder to ask you to sign a contract or purchase agreement before he sells the puppy to you. Usually the gist of the contract is that you agree to care for the welfare of the puppy, and often it states that if for any reason you need or wish to part with the puppy, even when it is fully grown, then you must give first refusal to the breeder. There may be other clauses, for instance requesting that you attend training classes or show the dog, but these are difficult for the breeder to enforce should you choose not to do so.

In most cases the contract is drawn up for the benefit of the dog and, as long as the dog is enjoying a good lifestyle and is not causing or suffering any problems due to the purchaser's negligence, then the breeder will be content.

registration in the UK

If the puppy is being sold as a pedigree dog with papers, you should make sure that the breeder has or intends to register the litter and individual puppies with The Kennel Club, and that this registration will be passed to you. It is not unusual for the documents not to have come through before the young pup goes to its new home, but you need these documents and

In this family of Yorkshire Terriers, the grandmother is in the centre, surrounded by her children and grandchildren.

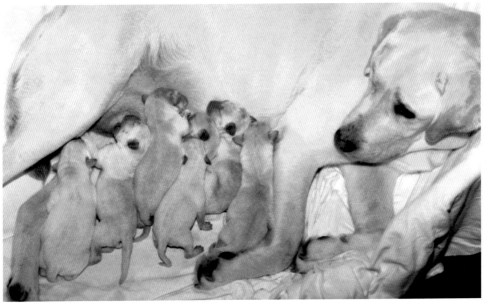

Always try to see the puppies together with their mother. A Labrador Retriever and her pups.

not simply a copy of the pedigree if showing or future breeding is important to you. If in any doubt, check with The Kennel Club to make sure the application is being processed.

Often puppy purchasers are dazzled by an impressive pedigree, sometimes full of red ink highlighting the champions within the lines. There is no guarantee that this pedigree is correct (although in most cases it is), and certainly you should be aware that, if there is no registration document, then the pedigree is worthless apart from as a point of interest. This does not necessarily mean that the dog is not any good; many dogs are sold without registration and make excellent pets and working dogs. But it is important that you realise and appreciate the implications.

The promise of papers to follow may well be written into a contract which the breeder gives you, or else you should get it in writing.

endorsements

There are different types of registration. In the United Kingdom, for instance, the breeder could choose to have the registration endorsed by The Kennel Club in several ways. 'Progeny not eligible for registration' means that unless the breeder sees fit to lift this ban, any pups your dog produces cannot be registered, and this devalues them considerably. If you were to allow the dog to breed, you would not gain much respect from others in the field.

The endorsement 'Not eligible for entry at shows, field trials, obedience classes, and working trials held under Kennel Club rules' may indicate that the pup has some fault which puts it outside the breed standard, and therefore the breeder does not want the pup seen in the show ring.

'Not eligible for issue of an export licence' is another very common endorsement, and this prevents you from selling the pup as a registered breed abroad.

The final endorsement is 'Name unchangeable'. The only change normally allowed is the addition of an affix should you have one. This endorsement prevents you adding an affix.

Always make sure you fully understand the breeder's intentions, otherwise you may be in for a disappointment. If you do not speak to the breeder about this, he may not deem it necessary to tell you (although he should), particularly if you had not expressed an interest in breeding or showing.

Note You may be buying a breed that can be registered with clubs that The Kennel Club recognises. For instance, a Border Collie pup may be ISDS registered. This means that it is registered with the International Sheepdog Society, and you will receive an official registration document to this effect. If this is the case, you will be able to apply for Kennel Club registration yourself should you wish to do so (although the breeder may have registered the pup with both KC and ISDS), because The Kennel Club recognises the ISDS as an official and well-established controlling body for the registration of stock.

unregistered dogs

If your dog does not have Kennel Club registration papers, all is not lost. In Great Britain, you can register the dog yourself but you are restricted to the Obedience and Working Trials register only. This means you may compete in KC-organised events such as Obedience, Agility and Working Trials, but cannot show your dog for its conformation in the breed ring except at exemption shows. Any progeny that your dog may go on to produce can be registered only in the same manner.

The good thing about this register is that any dog of any ancestry, including crossbreeds and mongrels, can be registered and therefore compete on equal grounds.

purchasing from a breeder

In most cases, buying a puppy is a simple business. The breeder will have already set a price based on various considerations, such as demand for dogs or bitches, and/or breeding and showing potential versus pet quality. Prices vary from breed to breed and line to line, the rarer breeds normally demanding higher prices. Dogs bred from current champions and show winning stock are also often more expensive than other lines.

If you are purchasing a pup from a litter that is in demand, then you may be asked to place a deposit to secure your purchase, and anything from 10–50% is normal, depending on the value of the pup. The balance is normally payable on collection (check whether the breeder requires cash or cheque).

Do not be surprised if the breeder has something to say about which puppy is more suitable for you, and in most cases this advice is worth heeding. Even if you are the first to be interested in the puppies, you may not be offered the 'pick of the litter', as your individual needs and situation should be taken into consideration.

Some breeders will want to keep a show-quality pup, hoping to find a keen show-going person to purchase it, or they may wish to keep it themselves to see if the pup makes the grade.

Most breeders will allow you to visit the pups many times before bringing home your choice, and you should take advantage of this to learn as much as you can about the pup and

The Kennel Club registration certificate.

its character. This also allows the pup to get to know you a little so that you are not a stranger when finally you take it from the safety of the nest. Sit amongst the puppies and try to get a feel of how they react and play. This will help you to relax when puppy comes home.

The best age to purchase your pup from a behavioural development point of view is about seven to eight weeks. At this age it will have had the benefit of interaction with its siblings, but still be in the socialisation stage of development, allowing it to take to new environments and situations with a minimum of trauma, and allowing you to start your social training when it is still very receptive.

Finally, make sure that you know what information you are getting with the pup regarding health, feeding, registration, pedigree, insurance and so on.

This form denotes that the animal can be shown only in Obedience, Agility and Working Trials.

International Sheep Dog Society registration form.

following up

The good breeder should follow up your pup's progress, not just to see if it is settling in, but to check how it is getting on physically and behaviourally and, of course, to find out about any achievements or problems.

Do not be afraid to contact the breeder at any time; good breeders will not class you as a nuisance as long as you are reasonable and do not ring at unsocial hours. Send pictures to the breeder and make sure he is kept informed of the pup's development. This helps the serious breeder to make decisions on what track to follow in any subsequent matings. He needs to know if the litter is worth repeating, or whether another line would be more appropriate.

buying an older pup

Although the best age to purchase a puppy is about seven to eight weeks, it is not unusual to see older pups for sale. Often this is because they have been kept by the breeder to see if they will make the grade as show or working dogs, and then they are offered for sale if they are not quite up to par. Occasionally the older pup is available because it just did not get sold, or someone booked it and then backed out. The reasons for this may or may not be anything to do with the quality of the pup.

A good breeder will have socialised the pup and worked hard on its temperament, and therefore you will be fortunate to get a good dog that will adjust well, and some of the training is already done for you. Sadly, there are all too many older pups that have not been

These Leonberger puppies are 'colour coded' with ribbons so that their individual progress can be followed by the breeder and prospective owners.

socialised, and have missed important events and experiences in their short lives. When this happens, it is an uphill struggle to get the pup to the standard that it might have attained had you taken it at seven weeks. This may result in a struggle for both dog and owner for the best part, if not the rest, of the dog's life.

Typically, pups that are not socialised are fearful, nervous and/or aggressive. They lack social graces with other dogs and people, and find it difficult to blend into a normal domestic regime. They may have been kennelled separately, and so not had the advantage of coming into contact with other dogs, or they may have been allowed to run with many others and not been given the essential opportunity to bond and enjoy human company. They may have met only their own kind and so other breeds come as a shock.

These problems are not something that they will grow out of without help. If you wish to try to change the dog's attitude and behaviour, you will have to apply positive behavioural modification programmes, and may well need expert help. You will need to be ultra-patient, and realise that it is not the pup's fault that it is behaving as it is.

puppy assessments

Puppy assessments, or puppy aptitude tests, are an ideal way to look at the potential of a puppy. The reports offer no guarantees, but they can give you an idea of what to expect, what potential the pup may have, and how well it reacts to and recovers from stress. There are many factors that will have an effect on the pup's reactions at this age, so ideally the tests should be carried out by more than one tester and on different days, and then the scores analysed and an average worked out. In practice, this seldom happens. Breeders should learn to observe and test behavioural reactions, as it is they who will spend most time with the pups. Although independent testers are more impartial (usually), the breeder should be able to predict the pup's result accurately, and use an independent tester to put the pup in a new situation and to confirm the findings. Breeders can use the tests to assess the pup's development over a period of time, and then work on its individual failings or strong points to bring out the best in it. The more pups you watch and interact with, the better you get at predicting potential. Things that can affect the results of tests can range from recent stresses and frights or hierarchy battles between the litter mates, to fatigue, hunger, a full bladder, and so on.

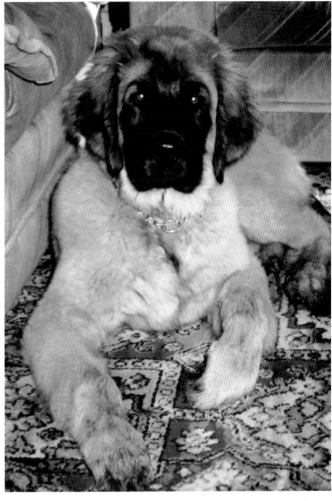

In less than five months, the little bundle of fluff opposite will grow to be as large as this!

I observed a well-balanced litter that reacted severely as a result of a rather rushed and unsympathetic tattooing session. I had been monitoring the pups' behaviour since their birth, and testing regularly since the age of four weeks. The pups were developing well and traits could be identified and developed quite early. One pup that previously had recovered well following mild trauma reacted very badly after being tattooed. He had been outgoing, active, people-friendly, and an ideal candidate for a working dog. His only minor failing was a low pain threshold. Following the tattoo, he became withdrawn and frightened of new things and of people, and his sole wish was to get back to the safety of his siblings. The breeder was able to work on this pup and help him to recover, but it was a long time before he regained his former character qualities. Another pup, who had been rather reserved anyway, became even more withdrawn and found it difficult to forgive.

This is not to say that breeders should not have pups tattooed, but that they should make sure that the tattooist is compassionate and they themselves must be willing to spend time in recovering the pups' confidence.

The trauma of other potentially painful experiences, such as removal of dew claws, does not have a lasting effect on behaviour, because these procedures are carried out at an early age when the pup's pain receptors are underdeveloped, and it is not in the socialisation or transitional period of its behavioural development.

The bold puppy may not be suitable for you – puppy assessments can help.
Photographs of Border Collie pups above and on page 32 by Sue Domun

A large part of the pup's development is affected by its environment and the mental and physical experiences that it has. However, if a pup is assessed accurately by an experienced person, the analysis can be used and referred to as the pup develops to explain and help prevent problems, as well as to channel and encourage correct and desirable behaviour.

There are various adaptations of the tests which, I believe, were first devised for the testing of potential guide dogs. Usually each pup is tested individually, out of sight of its litter mates, mother and any other animal that it has associated with. The test should be done in a place that is unfamiliar to the puppy, and the tester should handle the pup gently and with compassion throughout the tests. Ideally, the tester should not be familiar to the puppy.

The best age for a useful assessment is around seven weeks, but some of the tests can be done carefully as early as four weeks. Advice is then given to the breeder on individual care of the puppies to help bring out the best, and problem areas, if any, that should be worked on. To gain any benefit from early testing, the breeder must be very dedicated and prepared to spend time working on each puppy individually.

A brief outline of the tests

1   Isolation
The pup is placed in the room and the tester steps back out of immediate sight of the pup for 30 seconds.

2   Social attraction
The pup is placed in the room, the tester then encourages the pup to come towards him.

3   Following
The pup is encouraged to follow the tester.

4   Restraint
The pup is rolled on its back and held in position for up to 30 seconds. The time is recorded if it starts to struggle or show adverse reactions, such as biting or growling.

5   Noise sensitivity and investigation
A wind-up or drag toy that makes noises is placed in front of the pup – its reaction and inclination to investigate is noted.

6   Social dominance
The pup is picked up from behind and then stroked from head to tail.

7   Elevation dominance
The pup is lifted off the ground and held under its belly for 30 seconds. Sometimes the pup is placed at the top of a shallow ramp and the tester observes how it works out the way to get down, and its response to the elevated position.

8   Touch sensitivity
The skin between the pup's toes is gently squeezed with increasing pressure.

9   Play drive and possession
A soft and interesting toy is moved around temptingly in front of the pup, and it is encouraged to play and tug. The toy is released and the tester waits to see if the pup wants to carry on playing or goes off with the toy.

10 Gun shot
The pups are observed in small groups and a cap gun is fired approximately 15 metres away from them.

chapter *three*

Assessments help to identify a puppy's potential and character. Photograph by Tracey Jasper

In each of the tests the tester looks to see how the animal reacts, whether it is frightened, interested, resigned, aggressive, struggling, attentive, tense, blasé, and so on.

The results of these tests are graded and then evaluated, and herein lies the skill: the ability of the tester and breeder to consider what they have witnessed, and then to make relevant reports to help the new owners to bring out the best in their pups. Of course, there are great differences within breeds, and the results would be useless if consideration was not given to the genetic structure of the dog, both physically and behaviourally.

There is much debate on the value of these tests, as often dogs turn out quite differently to the predictions made on the report. This could, in part, be due to the owner's tendency not to use fully the information gained. If a pup is described as having good training potential, the handler must also have the ability to bring this out and control it. Dominant and submissive behaviours are also very misleading, as much of this behaviour is governed by hormonal changes and, of course, is dependent on the way that the animal is allowed to develop within the social structure of the home and external environment.

Some assessments are carried out for specific purposes, such as breed surveys, potential for obedience, agility, assistance work or hunting. When this is done, the emphasis of the report will concentrate on that issue, so it is worth asking the purpose of the assessment. If you want a specific type of character, and you are planning well ahead, ask the breeder to instruct the tester to bear this in mind when assessing the litter.

You cannot use your aptitude test as a crutch to lean on when things do not go according to plan. Nor can you blame the tester for what you may class as inaccuracies in the description of your pup. So much of the dog's behaviour is learnt that it is very difficult to evaluate the end result, and the test purpose is only to evaluate a potential. The results have been largely accurate in the dogs that I have tested, certainly in the eyes of myself and the breeders, but the new owner who is not quite so knowledgeable may be less inclined to agree on some aspects.

In pups that I have assessed and kept for myself and my friends (although I do appreciate that this is relatively very few for statistical purposes), all have delivered the type of attitude and temperament predicted, but only with the addition of channelling, training, correct handling and environment.

breed assessments

Some breeders will assess or have the litter assessed for its potential in the show ring. As with behavioural assessments, there are so many variables that it can make the results disappointing. The conformation of a good dog can be ruined by incorrect feeding; over- or

under-feeding of certain nutrients, vitamins, minerals and calcium. Also much damage can be done by over- or under-exercising, allowing the pup to go up and down stairs, long periods on unsuitable floor surfaces, or by accidents. Some dogs, particularly the larger breeds, may encounter problems due to rapid growth, and may appear to be out of proportion or even develop limps due to the growth in bone versus muscle ratio.

It is also a fact that the assessment is purely an opinion, and one assessor's vision of the perfect specimen of the breed may not be that of the next person or 'expert'. Everyone should be following the breed standard, but often there is much room for interpretation within these rules. It is not always easy to determine how the pup will develop by assessing at such an early age, but it is fun trying. Some assessors and breeders, however, are very good at spotting the potential winner.

Your puppy may choose you! Photo by Sue Domun

4 choosing the right puppy

Once you have done your ground work and located a good breeder, if at all possible go to see the stud dog before you visit, and fall in love with, the puppies. The father will pass on many traits to your puppy, and it is important that you like him as much as the mother. Most stud dog owners will be pleased to talk to you, as long as you are polite, explain why you want to see the dog, and offer to see them at a convenient time and place.

A young pup has blue eyes, but these change by the time it is ready to leave the litter. 'Quilty', aged four months, bred by Mrs H. Meyer and owned by Mrs L. Turtill.

If you have found a keen breeder, you may even have the benefit of puppy assessments of one kind or another (see chapter 3), so now the time has come to make some choices. If you have set ideas about what you would like to achieve with your new pup, it is a good idea to discuss this with the breeder before you get too emotionally taken by the cute little pup hiding in the corner. The breeder should be able to identify pups that have shown the sort of traits that you want.

physical and mental condition

It is of utmost importance that you try to choose a pup that is sound in every way. This is very difficult and almost impossible to be sure of, but having an idea what to look for will help you to avoid mistakes.

The pups in the litter should not be unduly frightened or nervous of your presence. Puppies learn a lot about the environment from their mother, so it is preferable to see the bitch interacting with the pups to make sure that she is neither aggressive nor agitated with them. For this, it is best to try to plan

choosing the right puppy

ahead and see the puppies before they are weaned. (Beware of breeders who won't allow this – what are they hiding?) Most breeders are pleased for visitors to come along and see the litter, at the very least from approximately two to three weeks onwards, as this helps to socialise the pups with other people.

You should be asked to observe hygiene precautions, such as using a disinfectant foot dip, washing your hands before touching the pups, visiting in clean clothes that have not come into contact with other dogs or dirty areas, and not petting any other dogs on the way. This is normal and shows that the breeder understands and is trying to minimise infection risks.

It is not always possible to see the bitch with the puppies if you leave viewing them until they are ready to leave the breeder. Many breeders will have separated the mother and her pups so that the bitch can get back into condition more rapidly, especially if she is a show bitch.

Once you are happy about the mental stability of the litter and bitch, look at the condition of the animals, and the cleanliness and suitability of the surroundings. You may see the odd damp patch or little pile of faeces, but there should not be a great amount. Certainly you should not see old faeces or urine stains, and any 'little accidents' should be fresh ones.

Now look at the physical condition of the pups.

Follow hygiene rules – but then you should be able to feel 'at home' with the pups.

Weight They should not be so thin that you can see every rib, but on the other hand they should not be over-fat. Gone are the days when we believed that 'a fat puppy is a healthy puppy'. As with human babies, we now know it is better to have everything in proportion, so that no undue stress is put on developing joints and organs.

Skin The skin should be clear and clean with no sores or signs of parasites. You may see red spots on the pup's tummy which could indicate that it has been bitten by fleas, and you may see tiny, dark-red specks of dirt which are flea droppings. In bad cases you may even see a flea if you run your fingers through the fur around the neck. In country areas you may also see sheep ticks. These are tiny insects that bury their heads in the skin, and may cause infection.

Coat The coat should be clean, free from dirt and scurf, and well groomed. It depends on the breed of dog whether or not it should be shiny. The fluffy coat of a puppy often lacks real

The whole litter should be settled and content.   Photograph by Caroline Bell

shine, but a healthy coat should neither separate in ridges, nor stand away from the skin in an unnatural manner, nor should it be dull. There should be no bald patches or crusted areas.

Eyes Eyes should be clear, bright and alert and free from discharge. Check that both are the same colour, as in some breeds it is not uncommon to have one blue and one brown eye (wall-eyed). In some breeds it is acceptable or even desirable, but in many it is not, and not everyone likes to see it. The eyes of very young puppies are a bluish colour, but by the time the pups are ready to leave the litter, they will be turning to the correct colour.

Ears Turn back the ear flaps and look and smell inside. The ears should be clean and free from excessive wax. If the pup has been tattooed recently you may see some green, but don't worry as this will wear off, and you should be able to read the identification number.

Mouth Open the mouth and look at the teeth and the type of bite. Look for signs of undershot and overshot jaws. This is acceptable in some breeds, but in most it is not. Teeth should be clean, strong and sound with no signs of decay. There should be no drooling or frothing around the pup's mouth.

Bone structure Obviously bone structure will vary depending on the breed but, having said that, everything should be in the correct proportion and the bones should not be unduly frail or bulky. Any bowing of the legs or enlarged joints could be a sign of rickets caused by poor feeding. There should be no signs of cow hocks (hocks turned in), or 'Queen Anne legs' (toes turned out) as the pup stands. Its movement should be smooth and free. Whatever the breed, the pup should have the appearance of being a sturdy little animal.

There are some defects that can be seen even by the novice.

Dew claws   Look at the legs and check if there are dew claws. In most breeds it is considered a fault to have dew claws on the hind legs and most breeders have them removed when the pup is a few days old. (In some breeds such as the Pyrenean Mountain Dog, it is a desirable trait, so check with the breed standard.) Some breeders remove front dew claws too, especially in the case of working dogs, as it helps to prevent accidents later on because the dew claws are very prone to being caught.

Umbilical hernias are another common detectable defect. A hernia shows itself as a lump on the abdomen where the umbilical cord would have been attached. It is common in some breeds, rare in others. The defect can be a hereditary problem, but sometimes it is caused by stress on the umbilical cord at birth. In many instances, even a vet cannot tell which is the case. A very small lump may become less obvious as the pup grows, but larger lumps, and those that grow with the dog, are more of a problem and may require surgery at a later date, especially if the dog is to be bred.

The world is a big place when you get out in it.   Photograph by Julie French

You will need lots of stamina to keep up with these Husky pups as they mature.

Cleft palate is a defect normally identified by the breeder or the vet, and most affected puppies are humanely destroyed within days if not hours of birth, as they have great difficulty eating. A slight case may go undetected by the breeder, so always open the pup's mouth and check that the palate is intact (see also chapter 19).

working or show potential

If you want a good working dog for obedience or agility, then you should look for a dog with plenty of 'spirit' and 'go'. It will be happy to run after toys, be pleasantly stimulated by human voice and touch, and have the drive to keep going when others want to lie down and sleep. It may score as moderately dominant in a character assessment, although this is not crucial and other traits should also be taken into account. In fact, it is helpful if it is a little on the sensitive side, but not too much so.

Do not choose the dog that plays only with its litter mates, or is not interested in a gently-moving rag. It may make a good working dog eventually, but you have a head start with a dog with a more positive attitude. On the other hand, if you want to work your dog, but are relatively new to training, then the dog that is obsessively keen to play may be a little too much for you to handle.

The show dog also needs plenty of spirit to stand alertly and confidently in the breed ring and it helps, but is not essential, if it is easily 'switched on' by toys or titbits. Breeds such as the German Shepherd have to spend long periods of time gaiting (running) around the ring. If you are going to handle the dog in the ring, you will have to build up lots of stamina yourself!

The puppy who has good conformation is not always easy to spot. If it were, all the breeders would own all the champions! Having said that, when the pup is approximately six

choosing the right puppy

or seven weeks old, its body should be compact and everything in proportion. It is often more difficult to spot good potential later, because the pup may become out of proportion as it grows, and many breeds appear ungainly during this time. Once mature, these 'ugly ducklings' often turn into real 'swans'.

Remember to make sure that the pup you are purchasing has suitable Kennel Club or other registration for the purpose you require.

tails or not

Many breeders nowadays decide not to have their pups docked, that is, their tails cropped off, because they do not see it as necessary, or they consider it a barbaric act. Others opt to go with tradition and find a sympathetic vet to dock the puppies when they are a few days old. In the United Kingdom, it is against the veterinary Code of Practice to dock puppies, and it is illegal for a lay person to do it. Breeders who want their pups to be docked often give specific reasons for doing so, such as the problem of working dogs getting their tails caught up in undergrowth whilst they are working. I'll leave the moral view up to you. From a behavioural point of view it is far better for the dog to have a tail, because so much of the dog's body language is given by its tail. The height and position, the frequency of the sway or wag are all indicators to the dog's state of mind and it makes it far easier for humans and, more especially, other dogs to read it.

Some breeds have the opposite problem in that selective breeding has produced an unnaturally high tail carriage, as in the case of the Samoyed. To add insult to injury, this breed

Boxer puppies with docked tails.

possesses a sticking-up coat that signals piloerection (hackles up) to other dogs. Many dogs with unnatural characteristics suffer behavioural problems that could have been avoided, had they not been giving off incorrect or false body language signals to other dogs. The dog suffers from this, but so does the owner. If you have such a dog, select its playmates carefully as it matures to prevent it from learning incorrect behaviour due to the actions of the other dogs with which it comes into contact.

In the United Kingdom, other operations to change the appearance of the dog, for instance cropping of ears (apart from when done for health reasons), is illegal.

the family pet

If you want your pup to be a good all-round family pet, then you need to choose one that is not extreme in any way, perhaps on assessment scoring a little on the submissive rather than dominant side. It certainly should not be a fearful type. It will be moderately sensitive and make a good recovery from trauma. It should be easy-going, friendly and generally should hold its tail level and wag it frequently, particularly when touched or spoken to. (Of course, tail carriage may be misleading in dogs who naturally carry the tail high, so this must be taken into account.) The ears should be alert, and yet the facial expression should not show too much obsession.

It is not necessarily a good idea to choose the puppy that comes away from the group first and thrusts itself upon you. You may feel that you have been chosen by the pup and be flattered by its attention, and in some cases this pup will be fine for you. However, be aware, it may well turn out to be a rather strong or dominant character, and for some a little too much to handle.

Neither should you choose the one who hides away in corner; you may feel sorry for this pup, but once again it may have problems. It may be over-sensitive, over-submissive, and/or fearful. You may be capable of overcoming these problems, but it is hard work even for an experienced person to reshape a dog with extremes of behaviour at any age. It is far better

choosing the right *puppy*

if you do not have the problems to contend with in the first place. The ideal pet will also make a good all-round working dog (if that is what it is bred for), provided that you do not expect it to be extreme, or work obsessively.

breeding potential

If you are hoping ultimately to breed from your puppy, you are indeed looking a long way ahead and you must appreciate that there are no guarantees that the puppy you are purchasing today will be of good enough quality to breed from in the future. Genetics is a very

complex subject, and even the experts can make mistakes or have to deal with a problem that is totally unexpected. Having said that, there are many things that you can do that will help you to choose a dog with good breeding potential.

First, do your homework and make sure that the line you are purchasing from is of sound quality and any defects are well-documented so that you can make a realistic decision. Much of this is covered in chapters 2 and 3.

Make sure that you know as much as possible about the breed, including the physical and temperamental development, as well as any hereditary problems. Study genetics, at least on a basic level, so that you can have a reasonable idea whether or not what you are being told is feasible.

With regard to the individual that you choose from the litter there are a few things to look out for. In small or toy breeds you should choose a good-sized bitch to help avoid birthing problems. You should avoid purchasing from a breeder who does not allow you to

The ideal family pet should be friendly and easy-going. The ever-popular Retriever often possesses these qualities.
Photograph by Kathy Dorfgar

see the bitch with the litter, as he may be hiding a nervous or severe mother. The severity with which the bitch chastises her pups will have a bearing on the pup's future life and especially on her capabilities as a mother.

41

dog or bitch?

Choosing the sex of your puppy can sometimes be as difficult as choosing the individual or deciding on a breed. Really it depends on your individual requirements and aspirations. If all you want is a family pet, and you have no other dogs, then it depends on what you prefer, but make plans to get your pup neutered as soon as it is old enough.

On the whole, males tend to be a little (in some cases quite a lot) larger than females of the same breed. A male sometimes has more strength of character, and this can be more difficult to deal with in some breeds. Early neutering helps to keep this at bay, and often takes the edge off. Dominance is both learned and inherited.

Castration actually has little effect on

A dominant pup needs training.

dominance, as the brain is masculinised shortly after birth by a surge of the hormone testosterone. A further surge comes at puberty and this is why early castration can have some preventative effect, but it should not be used as a prop. Bitches sometimes have a sweeter nature, but do not be fooled, they can be quite strong-minded if not handled correctly. Dominant canines, that is, dogs that display dominance to humans, tend to be male. Together with fellow behavioural consultants, I certainly find that the vast majority of dogs with dominance problems are male, but we do see some females as well.

If you already have a dog then the situation is a little more complex. The

Mowgli, a Tibetan Terrier. Photograph by A Patterson

choosing the right *puppy*

combination least likely to cause problems is to acquire a dog of the opposite sex so that you have a male and female living together. The characteristics of any dog you already have must be taken into account and, although you may be lucky and the two become great friends, don't bank on it. If your first dog is quite a strong character and does not take to being pestered, then you should go for a more submissive dog. This will give you a head start on keeping the social gap wide. Most dogs have a few arguments as the younger animal develops, and they learn and at times challenge, or have challenged, their place in the hierarchy. Two males together are often less problem than two females as the hierarchy, once set, is more stable. Bitches tend to be more possessive, which may lead to aggressive behaviour irrespective of social ranking.

Bringing in a young puppy is usually easier than introducing two adult dogs. The pup learns as it goes along and to start with does not pose a threat to the adult dog. The larger dog usually assumes the alpha role if of the same breed and tendency, but with two different types it is not uncommon to find that the smaller and often more feisty dog becomes more dominant.

Finally, don't be afraid to decide against all the pups if you feel that you don't like any of them, or they do not suit your needs and expectations. This is not an easy decision to make when faced with those cute little bundles, but you are making a commitment to an animal that will be reliant on you for the next 10–16 years, so you must be as sure as possible of yourself and your choice.

Tara. Photograph by Caroline Bell

behavioural *development*

In order to understand your puppy, it is of paramount importance that you understand its development, not just from the physical aspect but from the behavioural point of view.

Our domestic dog has evolved from the wolf through natural and human selection, but no matter how different some breeds may appear, there is still a strong element of wolf instinctive behaviour and influence which dictates how the dog reacts. The canine in your living room reacts in a very similar way to the young wolf in the wild in that it has the ability to adapt to the environment, and relate to the things and other animals around it, be it canine or otherwise.

Food plays a major part in shaping and dictating the dog's behaviour patterns, as does the drive to reproduce. The availability of both these all-important motivators has a marked effect on the dog's behaviour and struggle for supremacy. As it goes thorough the developmental process, the pup tries out, practises and develops the skills that it will need to aid its own survival and that of its progeny.

The puppy is extremely influenced by its environment from the moment that it is born and even before. The behavioural development can be broken down into seven different phases: the prenatal period, the neonatal period, the transitional period, the socialisation period, the juvenile period, the adolescent period and adulthood. Each period of the dog's development holds separate and yet linked factors, and trauma at the wrong time can have lasting effects. The development periods are first measured in weeks, and later in months, but this serves merely as a guide line. Pups vary, often quite remarkably, from these parameters. Sometimes differences will be observed individually or within breeds, but variations can also be related to individual circumstances surrounding the litter.

the prenatal period

Research shows that there can be an influence on eventual behaviour and development from factors taking place before the pup is born. Proper nutrition, fitness and warmth have been shown in studies on rats to have a marked effect on the babies. Similar studies on nutrition in pregnant cats have shown great differences in the intelligence, learning ability and capability to hunt effectively in the resulting progeny. And, of course, we know that prenatal care in humans is of paramount importance. Therefore, sensible breeders take care when preparing a bitch for conception and during her pregnancy, avoiding unnecessary drugs, chemicals, X-rays, inappropriate nutrition, and stress. They make sure that the bitch gets adequate exercise and nutrition.

Each pup has its own set of genes to influence eventual behaviour. Because of this, some dogs are predisposed to adapt or tackle certain aspects of their life better than others, but the care you take during all your dog's life stages will help to ensure good mental and physical health.

behavioural *development*

The fun starts now. A family of Labrador Retrievers photographed by Ms D Jones

the neonatal period

This period covers the first two weeks of the pup's life. The pup is completely dependent on its mother during this time. It spends its time sleeping and eating. Its brain is maturing. The things that the pup experiences from now and for the next 12 weeks have a marked effect on its whole life and its ability to deal with things. Early gentle handling helps it to develop and is good for its emotional balance. Almost all the social interaction will be with the mother only. The pup is sensitive to external temperature, touch, pain and taste, but is unable to regulate its own temperature. The pain receptors start to come into force after a few days, starting at the head and working their way down the body. Towards the latter part of this period the pup's eyes and ears start to open, but it is not until the next important stage that it responds to light, movement and loud noise.

the transitional period

This is the period when the pup really becomes aware of its surroundings. From two to four weeks, the pup goes from complete dependency to acquiring some of the skills that give it a degree of independence. It begins to walk rather than crawl, can go backwards as well as forwards, and even begins to lap milk. Some bitches regurgitate food for the pups, as the wolf would have done. Many do not do this sufficiently, if at all, and in a domestic situation the human 'mother' takes over the feeding, so beginning the weaning process. The pup reacts to movement and sounds, recognises people and, towards the end of the transitional period, it starts to show other behaviours such as barking, growling, tail wagging, raising of a paw and play. It develops the ability to urinate and defecate outside the nest.

the socialisation period

During this period the fun really starts for pup, breeder and, if he is around, potential new owner. The period, sometimes termed the 'critical period' due to its influence on future behaviour, covers from four to 12–16 weeks. At the beginning of this period, the pup has relatively well-developed sensory and motor skills, its brain is developed and it is ready for learning in a more complex way. It is becoming equipped to deal with its environment. There is a gradual progression in the dog's ability, and it learns to deal with new experiences in the safety of the nest and surrounding area. The bitch spends less time with the pups, naturally reducing the amount of milk that the pups can take, therefore encouraging them to eat more solid food. The pup learns how to interact with its litter mates and other animals that it comes into contact with and, during the early part of this period, it approaches new objects, humans, dogs, other animals and particularly things that move, with great interest.

Through play the puppy learns how to control biting, about prey-killing skills, and about acceptable behaviour within the group as a result of interaction with the litter, with the mother and, indeed, with other animals and objects that it meets. It learns the consequence of its actions and reactions. It learns about dominance and submission, and all the levels in-between.

Play is a most important part of growing up, and animals that play are more highly developed, intelligent and easier to train, because play leads them into more situations which they have to deal with. Pups denied play can develop strange behaviours such as self-mutilation, they don't learn as well as they should, they are shyer and reluctant to explore.

behavioural *development*

After this period of adjustment and learning, the pup has a built-in security system to prevent it from coming to harm. In the wild, once it has reached an age when it is able to leave the nest confidently, it would not be a good idea for the pup to be over-familiar with things or animals that it does not understand. Out in the big wide world, if you have not been told about 'this thing' then it could be a predator, and therefore you should give it a wide berth or risk the possibility of getting eaten!

Puppies isolated, deprived of sufficient social contact, or having had bad experiences during this all-important time, can exhibit behaviour that is difficult to deal with in later life, such as fear, hyper-aggression, inhibited behaviour, and inability to learn. They do not learn to inhibit the bite, and may be difficult to control in many situations. Pups deprived of canine company will be very human-oriented, and prefer human company to canine. This may seem desirable in some situations, but unfortunately the animal may well react in a fearful or aggressive way when it does come into contact with other dogs, and a bitch often makes a poor mother.

During the neonatal period, pups spend their time eating and sleeping.

Breeders and new owners can help the pup by introducing it to a wide range of things. For example, other animals, vacuum cleaners, hair dryers, children, people of both sexes, people in hats, tastes, smells, aerosols, umbrellas, different textures and floor coverings, air changes, temperatures, being handled and groomed, and much more, all help to make the pup confident. It is possible to make the dog so blasé to novel experiences that it reacts well to almost every new and changing situation. Stimuli should not be introduced in such a way that the pup becomes fearful, as this will be counter-productive, although it is good for the pup to experience and recover from some minor traumas to help it to deal with adversity in the future. The pup that is 'wrapped in cotton wool', as it were, and only allowed to have good experiences, may develop a different set of behavioural problems. Pups will also be influenced by the mother's reaction to various situations. For example, if the bitch is frightened when people approach this will be learned by the puppies, and they too will be affected.

the juvenile period

The juvenile period overlaps the socialisation period. It can start at about 10–12 weeks and stretches to the emergence of sexual maturity. During the juvenile period the pup practises and perfects its motor skills, learns what behaviours to use and where, and the relevance or effect of that behaviour on a particular situation. It is learning and developing its position in the hierarchy. At the age of approximately 10 weeks the ability to learn is just about fully developed, but by 12 weeks the influence of what the pup has already learned slows down its ability to take in new tasks. The concentration span of the juvenile dog is much shorter than that of the adult, and needs to be developed before more difficult tasks can be taught.

Males learn to raise or 'cock' their leg to urinate and this marks the end of the juvenile period. The timing of this varies depending on the individual. It is often quite late in low-ranking animals. Males mature slowly and it is an on-going procedure with the amount of testosterone (male hormone responsible for male behaviour and the production of sperm) gradually increasing. The young male will become interested in on-heat bitches as early as four months of age, but it will not be able to have a fertile mating until it is about seven or eight months old.

Transitional period: feeding time is messy as the pups learn to eat soft food.

behavioural *development*

Introduce the pup to all sorts of things.   Shetland Sheepdog photographed by Mrs J Margetts

There is a much more sudden change from juvenile to young adult in females. This usually comes with the first season, and therefore the timing is dependent on the bitch as an individual. Some bitches have their first season (oestrous cycle) at approximately six months. Others can be as old as 18 months before they cycle. Often the first season is not as obvious as subsequent ones, with relatively little of the characteristic vulva swelling and bleeding. The behaviour of the young bitch is often the give-away as she shows a sudden interest in male dogs.

adolescence

Adolescence is a period in the dog's life sometimes neglected from the point of view of importance as a life stage. It is the period, as in humans, when the dog is maturing and becoming a sexually-mature young adult with a juvenile's mind. Many breeders experience the results of the out-of-control 'teenager', when suddenly they hear from a puppy owner whose little darling has turned into a hooligan overnight. Other owners make sudden, desperate appeals to every dog trainer, behavioural consultant and vet in an effort to gain control of their beast. Often the dog displays almost angelic qualities in the hands of others, but is a real problem with the owner and at home. Some owners take this personally or cannot cope with the situation. This is one of the most common stages at which dogs are re-homed. The problem does not happen overnight; there is a gradual build up, and the dog's maturing body and mind must be controlled and stimulated effectively if it is to remain in the control of the humans.

In order for you to 'survive' this stage of your dog's development, it is important first of all to acknowledge its existence. In many ways, the dog is like an adolescent human. The key with dogs, as with humans, is give them sufficient stimulation to occupy both mind and body

These pups may look as innocent as angels – but beware as they reach adolescence.

in order to render them fulfilled. If the dog had been in the wild as were its forefathers, the time would have come for it to be out practising its newly-acquired hunting skills, or working on its powers of seduction and status-building. In the home, it has learned the basics of life in domesticity, but now what? It needs to have more to do than hang around waiting for something to happen. When the canine adolescent starts tearing around the house to rid itself of excess energy, urinates on the door frame or mounts the two-year-old human, spooks over silly things or shows aggression, we quite naturally find this a problem. We should remember that in the wild the young dog would have been running around in the fields and playing with its peers, just as human teenagers may 'lark around', investigate things previously off limits, and seem over-boisterous to the older 'been there, done that' generation.

Even if you have been vigilant and followed a training programme, your pup may hit adolescence and become a raving nutcase – or worse! At the onset of training the dog is over-awed by the strange world that it finds itself in, and looks to you for guidance. However, with the onset of puberty, evolution orders that it must become more independent and prepare to deal with life alone. Now there is a conflict between the young body and mind, combined with the restraints of those who set the rules.

The young adolescent finds it very difficult to concentrate. It is bigger, stronger, and life holds so much in store that it is a bore being tied to mother's apron strings. Think back to how you felt yourself! In order to maintain control, you must do more than merely follow a series of training exercises and social training. The dog needs to know that you are in control, and maintain that need to look to you for guidance and security. We do not want our canine to grow up taking control of its own life, because it will need to live as part of ours.

adulthood

Dogs develop into mental and physical adulthood at differing stages, depending on the type of dog. Some dogs, notably large breeds, do not become fully mature until they are two to three years old. It is not impossible to train an older dog, and sometimes in experienced hands the older dog gives quicker results than does a puppy. You can often achieve good results with an adult dog, even if it has some behavioural problems, and it may be easier for the new owner to deal with those problems than the previous owner, who had allowed them to develop and become the norm. This is because the new owner does not allow the incorrect or inappropriate behaviours to happen, or when bad behaviours surface, he reacts immediately to stop them and prevent further recurrence. This phenomenon can be seen at dog schools where the instructor takes hold of an unruly dog and, with minimal effort on his part, turns the dog into an angel! The instructor's experience and ability to take control and react with his body language and mental attitude tells the dog many things straight away. Remember that the dog does not speak any human language, so words may not even be uttered by the good trainer. Coupled with perfect timing and good handling techniques, the instructor appears to have mystical powers over the canine.

to sum up

The best age to get your puppy is at about seven weeks. It has had the benefit of the interaction with the rest of the litter, learned to accept new situations and is still in that critical socialisation period so you can introduce it to new situations in your home and local environment. In tests carried out by the Guide Dogs for the Blind, it was found that dogs that left the breeding kennels at six weeks stood as much, if not a better, chance of becoming guide dogs than the ones that went over 12 weeks old.

What sort of dog are you? asks the Leonerger and his Parson Jack Russell friend.

6 before puppy comes home

It is important to prepare for the arrival of your new puppy. It is not a toy, and it has real needs you must cater for. It is best to speak in detail with the breeder about the feeding and routines that the pup has been used to up until its final hours with the litter.

Buy the same food that the breeder has already used. Most breeders will give you a little to start you off, but make sure you have some more ready. Also items such as dishes, bedding and even secure fencing are often left to the last minute or forgotten and, if you are not careful, the new puppy arrives and plunges the whole household into chaos.

Therefore, make sure that the garden is puppy-proof; remember that at the moment the pup may be able to get through quite small gaps, but also remember how it will grow and save yourself added expense by planning for the future.

This innocent little pup can plunge the whole household into chaos. Photograph by Karen Rawlinson

After consulting the breeder about diet, and before the puppy arrives, make a list, and go shopping. Basic items include: food, two dishes, brush and comb, puppy collar and lead, small soft treats, bedding, safe training and chew toys. If you intend to have your dog in an indoor kennel or crate (which is a very good idea), organise this before it arrives as well. Do all your shopping before the puppy arrives so that you do not have to go out and leave it.

Before the puppy becomes part of your household, decide on designated bed areas, rules that you intend to implement, and how you intend to go about this. Think about your family and any other animals that you may have, consider their reactions to the new arrival, and how you are going to introduce them.

Any young children in the household need to be encouraged and educated to understand the needs of the puppy. They must be

Set rules for everyone to follow, or your 'little angel' will soon take over.

prevented from running around screaming, and learn to pick up toys that otherwise will end up as puppy chews! The introduction of a new puppy is bound to be exciting for children. However, they need to be aware of the fact that the puppy is an animal and not a toy or playmate in the human sense of the word, although of course they will have lots of fun together (see chapter 15).

Try to collect your puppy at a time when you will be able to devote a considerable amount of attention to it, such as during a holiday period. You will be able to get it into a good routine, attend to its needs in those early days, teach some basic training keywords, and get it accustomed to being alone before it has to be left for real.

chapter *six*

What to ask the breeder before you collect your pup

When was the pup born? . . . .

When was the pup last wormed? . . . .

When is the next dose due? . . . .

What type of worming compound was used? . . . .

Has the pup had any inoculations? . . . .

If so, what and when? . . . .

When is the pup next due to be inoculated? . . . .

What food is it on? . . . .

How long should it be kept on this food? . . . .

At what times is it accustomed to being fed? . . . .

How many meals is it on? . . . .

How much does it normally eat at each meal? . . . .

Has the pup been ill at all? . . . .

Has the pup had any minor operations, such as removal of dew claws? . . . .

Has the pup seen the vet for any other reason? . . . .

Is the pup tattooed or micro-chipped? . . . .

Is the pup insured? . . . .

Has Kennel Club registration come through or been applied for? . . . .

Will the pedigree be available when the pup is collected? . . . .

Is there to be a breeder's contract? If so, what will be included? . . . .

Will there be any endorsements/restrictions on its registration? . . . .

How should payment be made? . . . .

What sort of experiences has the pup already had? For instance:

       Has it met cats/other animals? . . . .

       Has it met children? . . . .

       Has it been in a car? . . . .

       Has it ever been alone? . . . .

My name should be 'Happy'.   Photograph courtesy of Mrs P Farey

Another important thing to consider is which veterinary surgeon you will use. Try to find one fairly close to home if you can. Ring the surgery, find out about appointment arrangements, and check what age your pup's first inoculation will be administered. The vet will probably want to see the pup straight away for a check up, and this is a good idea as you will then have a professional opinion and be told if there is anything that you should be aware of regarding the puppy's state of health.

There are some fun things to do as well, such as choosing a name, finding out about puppy groups and dog training classes and, most importantly, reading the rest of this book! It will be very helpful if you understand as much as possible about your new family member. There is much to learn about the rearing and training of the perfect puppy, but the more you read and take in, the more natural the whole thing will become.

checklist –
what to do before you collect puppy

- Find a suitable veterinary surgeon.
- Make sure your garden is puppy proof.
- Go shopping for: food, dishes, bedding, bed, crate, grooming equipment, training toys, safe chews, lead and collar.
- Find out about puppy groups, parties, classes.
- Decide on house rules: where it will sleep, which rooms it will be allowed in, whether it is allowed on furniture, and so on.
- Decide on a suitable toilet area.
- Decide on a name.

naming your pup

The naming of your puppy is quite an important business. It might seem easy to pick a name that you like or that seems to suit the pup, but your choice of names can affect how you and the pup are treated by others and even have a psychological effect on you!

Names have a tendency to go in types

according to the breed in question. For instance, I know many Boxer dogs named after sportsmen such as Bruno, Tyson and Frank. Other big breeds such as Rottweilers tend to get landed with names like Samson, King, Trojan or Saracen. German Shepherds are given names such as Prince. All of these names suggest a high-ranking position or a tough image and you must be careful that you do not get carried away with the subconscious meaning of the name. The most common, or should I say popular, names that I come across are Ben and Sam.

In the competitive dog world it is often a good idea to have a different name for your dog from those chosen by others. This helps to avoid confusion and is particularly useful in competitive obedience where the dog must pay attention to the handler all the time. If someone outside the ring is calling a dog with the same name as yours, it can be very distracting and may result in point loss.

It is also worth remembering that, whether in a competition, at home or in a public place, you may want to call the name from a distance. Therefore it is worth trying out names yourself to make sure that you find them easy to call. Some names feel uncomfortable when you say them in anything except normal speech, and you may even end up hurting your throat.

Double syllable names are often easier to call, and have a more pleasing ring, as are names ending in 'y', 'ie', or 'er' such as Jinty, Chessie, Kelly, Taffy, Kizzy, Chipper, Jasper.

Sheepdog owners have a tendency to prefer the use of more traditional single syllable names like Spot, Cap, Jyp.

Zoe the Welsh Corgi models what the well-dressed pup is wearing: a soft collar with identity disc. Photograph by Maria Carter

chapter six

changing the name

It is not uncommon to wish that you had chosen a different name or find yourself abbreviating the one you have chosen, or you may have inherited a name with the puppy that you just do not like. Don't worry if you decide to change, the dog will soon adjust. Simply start again, teaching it good associations with your chosen name. For example, at feeding time show the pup the food and precede your key words ('sit', and 'eat') with the new name. Likewise, at other times, such as play and walks, simply put in the new name before your key words (see chapter 17).

name choices

The choice of name is yours, but remember you could well be calling the name in public, or from your doorstep in your night clothes. Do you really want to call names like Willy, Precious, Cherub, Fee-Fee?

Here are a few names from my collection that you might like to consider for your pup:

A: Abbie, Adam, Addie, Alfie, Allie, Alma, Amber, Amigo, Amy, Andy, Annie, Angus, Archie, Arkle, Arnie, Arrow, Artie, Astra.

B: Badger, Balloo, Bambie, Banner, Barnie, Bart, Basil, Beckie, Ben, Benjie, Bella, Belle, Benson, Bertie, Berry, Bessie, Betty, Biba, Billy, Binty, Blaze, Blitz, Blue, Bracken, Bradie, Bramble, Bransby, Breeze, Brett, Britt, Bobbie, Bodie, Bonnie, Bowie, Brandy, Bruce, Buckle, Buddy, Buster, Buttons, Buzz.

C: Cable, Cadbury, Calypso, Cammy, Cap, Caper, Cara, Casey, Cash, Casper, Cassie, Cedar, Cindy, Charmer, Charlie, Chloe, Checker, Cherry, Chipper, Chips, Chocky, Chumly, Clarry, Cleo, Clint, Clyde, Codie, Copper, Cora, Corrie, Critter, Cracker, Craig, Crispin, Crofter, Crunchie, Crystal.

D: Daffy, Daisy, Daley, Dallas, Danny, Dancer, Dart, Dash, Davie, Dazzle, Dazzler, Deanie, Debbie, Decker, Deefa, Del, Digger, Dilly, Dirk, Disney, Dixey, Dolly, Donny, Dreamer, Duffy, Duke, Dusty, Dylan.

E: Echo, Eddie, Elkie, Elton, Elvis, Ella, Elliot, Ember, Emily, Emma, Ernie.

F: Fanta, Faye, Fergus, Fern, Fizz, Flash, Flax, Fleet, Flicker, Fluke, Flurry, Fly, Frankie, Frayer, Freckles, Freddy, Friday, Flower, Foxy, Fudge.

G: Gabbie, Gail, Garry, Glen, Gina, Gertie, Gerry, Georgie, Gemma, Gigi, Gilbert, Giles, Glimpse, Glint, Goldie, Greg, Griffin, Griff, Gus, Gwen, Gypsy.

H: Hamish, Harriet, Harris, Harry, Harvey, Heather, Hebe, Hector, Heidi, Henry, Herbie, Hero, Hester, Hughie, Hobie, Hobo, Holly, Homer, Honey.

I: Igor, Immy, Indy, Ingy, Inkie, Inko, Iris, Iska, Ismar, Issac, Ivor, Ivy, Izzak, Izzey.

J: Jacie, Jack, Jackie, Jade, Jake, Jamie, Janie, Jarnie, Jarna, Jasper, Jay, Jazz, Jeannie, Jenna, Jenny, Jemma, Jerry, Jessie, Jilly, Jimmy, Jingle, Jinntie, Jinny, Jockey, Jodey, Joey, Joker, Josey, Josh, Judy, Juno.

K: Kanga, Karla, Katie, Kassie, Keeta, Kellsa, Kelly, Kelpie, Keltie, Kenny, Kermie, Kerry, Kes, Kezzy, Kipper, Kim, Kiri, Kizzy, Kylie.

L: Lacie, Laddie, Lady, Larna, Larry, Lance, Lassie, Laurie, Layla, Lena, Lenny, Leo, Leon, Leroy, Lester, Letty, Levi, Lewis, Libby, Lindie, Lizzie, Logan, Lois, Loppy, Lucas, Lucky, Lucy, Lulu, Lyn.

M: Mac, Manny, Maggie, Magic, Magnum, Marcus, Mandy, Marty, Marvel, Mattie, Maxie, Mazzy, Meg, Meggie, Merrie, Micky, Micra, Micro, Midas, Midge, Milly, Milo, Minka, Mirk, Mischa, Misty, Molly, Monday, Monty, Moss, Mousey, Myth.

N: Nancy, Nat, Nattie, Nell, Nelly, Neppy, Nerry, Nessie, Nickita, Nicky, Nike, Nino, Nipper, Norton, Nuala.

O: Obbie, Offra, Olly, Omar, Oprah, Orvil, Oscar, Ossie, Otis, Otto.

P: Paddy, Panda, Pansy, Pashca, Patch, Pebbles, Peggy, Pepper, Pepsi, Penny, Percy, Perdie, Pete, Phoebe, Pip, Pippa, Piper, Pippin, Prue, Polly, Polo, Poppy, Pru, Pudsey.

Q: Quallie, Quanto, Quantro, Queenie, Quest, Quill, Quincy, Quintan, Quiver, Quiz, Quizzer, Quizzie.

R: Rabbie, Radar, Raffles, Raggs, Rascal, Red, Remus, Reno, Reo, Rickie, Rigby, Rigsby, Rilly, Rita, Ritz, Robbie, Rocket, Roddie, Rolly, Rorrie, Rosie, Rossie, Ross, Roxy, Rubble, Ruby, Ruffles, Rupert, Rummy, Ryan.

S: Sadie, Sammy, Sally, Sasha, Scoobie, Scot, Scottie, Sebbie, Shaddow, Sharda, Sheena, Sidney, Skie, Skipper, Smartie, Smudge, Snicker, Snoopy, Socksy, Solo, Sparkie, Sparkle, Speedy, Spike, Spicer, Star, Stella, Stricker, Sue, Sunny, Susie, Sweep.

T: Taffy, Tammy, Tamsin, Tango, Tara, Tarka, Tarn, Teddy, Tessa, Ticket, Tiffy, Tilly, Timmy, Tinker, Toby, Toffee, Thomas, Thomson, Tommy, Tonly, Tony, Tramp, Treacle, Trigger, Tristan, Trixie, Trudie, Truffle, Tucker, Turbo, Tweed, Twiggy, Twistie, Twister, Tyke, Tyson.

U: Uno, Urrie, Unie.

V: Verity, Vesta, Vicky, Victor, Vida, Vince, Vinny, Viv, Viva.

W: Walker, Wally, Wanda, Warren, Webley, Wembley, Wendy, Wesley, Whisper, Whitney, Whiz, Whoopi, Willow, Wills, Willy, Winner, Winny, Winston, Wizard, Woody, Woolfie, Woodrow, Wookie.

X: Xyagan, Xaneth, Xena, Xenia.

Y: Yappy, Yarna, Yarnie, Yasmin, Yega, Yippy, Yogal, Yogie, Yoko.

Z: Zack, Zak, Zanni, Zara, Zebby, Zecker, Zeros, Zeta, Zelda, Ziggy, Zimba, Zing, Zinna, Zinnia, Zippy, Zola, Zoro, Zowie.

essential
equipment

There are several items that are needed for the proper care, guidance and training of your new puppy. Some may seem obvious, some a little less so.

sleeping arrangements

Where your pup sleeps is important to its understanding of its position within the family. It is best that you do not allow the pup to sleep on your own bed, as this is telling it that it is on a par with you socially. From there, it is not very difficult for it to take that step up which places it, at least in its mind, above you in the hierarchy. This can lead to unwelcome problems of dominance and aggression, if not with you then with other members of the family who dare to come on or into your bed as well.

For the first few days it is often easier to have the pup in your bedroom with you, but keep it on the floor by your side in a special bed, box or crate. It will settle better and be easier to house train if its movement is restricted to a small area. Therefore, the best piece of equipment for sleeping and for restricting the dog's movements is a deep-sided box for small breeds or, better still for all breeds, a crate (see chapter 8).

Your pup needs to feel secure. Holly, a Cavalier King Charles Spaniel, aged 10 weeks. Photograph by Mrs J Chambers.

essential equipment

A bed made of plastic resists the chewing power of most pups.

You will need a crate big enough for the pup to lay down flat, taking into account the fact that you may well want to use the crate even when your dog is fully grown. Buy a fairly large crate, or enquire at your vet or local dog trainer about the possibility of renting one.

You will also need bedding – the best is good quality veterinary or medical bedding, the type that is sometimes used in hospitals as under-blankets to prevent bedsores and give added warmth. Pet owners can now buy these easily from good pet shops. It is easy to wash, and any little accidents soak through leaving the pup relatively dry. The bedding can be quite expensive, but it is worth spending that bit more if you want the best for your pup. Nothing in this line is anti-chew but, as bedding goes, pups seem less liable to chew this than other bedding.

If you feel your dog needs a bed, opt for a high-density plastic type. Once again these are easy to keep clean, and fairly chew resistant. The old-fashioned basketware beds look really good, but unfortunately are not very hygienic because they harbour dust and germs, and many pups love to chew the natural material that they are made from.

leads and collars

When you first get your puppy probably it will never have had a collar around its neck. The best sort to start with is of soft nylon, with a buckle fastening. This is cheap to buy, easy to clean, and gentle on the pup. To go with this you could purchase a matching lead or opt for something more substantial that will last for some time. You never need an old-fashioned choke or check chain to train your pup, and only if you make mistakes in your training will you have to consider any other form of neck, body or head wear.

A grooming table is a useful piece of equipment.

Later you may wish to consider using a special walking harness to walk your dog but, if you follow the techniques in the following sections, especially in chapter 17, you will be able to keep perfect control with a standard lead and buckled collar.

The important things to consider about your lead are:

- that it is soft on your hands,
- has a safe trigger-style fastener,
- is about 1.2m (4ft) long, and
- is strong enough to hold your dog.

There are many leads available that meet these criteria. Do not be tempted to buy a chain lead, as these are very harsh on your hands, and the noise they make is unpleasant and distracting for some more sensitive pups. Leads can be made of bridle leather, soft cotton webbing, or braided rope. What you are looking for is something fairly tough, and yet soft on your hands.

It is very useful to have an extending lead. This can be helpful when training your dog at a distance, giving you added control, and also it will give the dog a little more freedom when you are walking in an area where dogs must be kept on lead. Extending leads should only be used in areas where the dog's freedom will not interfere with others. If you are walking the dog in a public or populated area, the lead should be kept in the locked position, thus keeping the dog safely by your side.

A long line can help you to control the pup in the home and when it is running free, but this will not be needed until it is a little older and bolder. The idea is that the pup drags the line around behind it, giving you the instant control of being able to grab the end when you need to. However, if you follow the training procedures, it unlikely to be necessary.

toys as training aids

Toys are a most important part of your dog kit. They are one of your major training aids, and you should use toys as part of your daily routine (see chapters 11, 16 and 17).

The toys that you choose for your pup should be safe and strong, and at least some of them should be of the tug variety, that is, both you and the dog can hold on to them together. Ideal are Tug-a-balls or knots, rope coits, rubber rings, knotted ropes and knotted socks.

A toy with an audible sound, such as a squeaky ball, is good for teaching the dog to come to you. Buy a good quality toy, and do not leave it with the pup otherwise the squeak will not last for very long.

It is important that any toy that is to be thrown is not so small that it could get stuck in the dog's throat, and remember that what might be suitable for your pup while it is small could very soon become a dangerous object as it grows. Attach a solid rubber ball to a rope in the form of a tug-a-ball, so that you can pull it out of the dog's throat in the event of an accident. If you want a standard ball without a rope attachment, choose a soft ball that can be collapsed should it get caught in the dog's throat.

None of these toys are meant to be left with the dog for it to play with alone, to chew, or even simply take into its bed. They are training aids, and should be put away when you are not training the pup.

Caution: Invariably dogs love sticks that they or you find while out walking. Never throw sticks for your dog, as the danger is that they may land in the ground and the dog comes down on top of them, forcing the end through its palate or down the throat. Even the splinters can cause severe wounds.

toys as chews

Special chew toys have been developed to act as therapeutic devices which are safe to be left with the pup. These include items in the Nylabone range that have been impregnated with interesting flavours to keep the pup busy for hours, and have the added benefit of helping with canine dental hygiene and health.

A selection of Nylabone products. You are sure to find one that will suit your own pet.

On no account should you leave your pup with toys that are not designed specifically for chewing as these can cause all sorts of internal problems if ingested. Even toys that are labelled as 'non toxic' can cause problems – they may be non toxic but they are not meant to be eaten!

titbits

Titbits are another important part of your training kit. It might seem odd to include them in a list of equipment but, if used correctly, they are indeed essential items.

Titbits should be very small if they are to be of any use as training aids. The more palatable they are, the more effective they will be. It pays to have a selection so that if the dog gets too bored of one it can have another. While the pup is tiny, it is best to use soft treats in conjunction with training which can be eaten easily but, as the pup matures, you will be able to use crunchier varieties.

Save the tastiest morsels for the times that are potentially most difficult. For instance, on your first trip to the veterinary surgeon, take along some chopped cooked meat to feed the pup when it is on the vet's table.

canine hygiene

All dog owners should buy a suitable brush or comb to keep their pet's coat in good condition. To begin with, the pup's coat will be very soft, but it still needs grooming to keep it clean and free from debris. Grooming is also an important part of social training, and you should make

A Nylabone Dental Floss is both fun and good for your dog's teeth.   Photograph by Sue Domun

Good food, exercise, grooming and lots of tender loving care will help your puppy grow up to be a happy and healthy dog. West Highland Whites photographed by Robert Smith

sure that you can groom all parts of your dog's body. If your dog is a breed that needs special grooming then contact your breeder or grooming specialist straight away and ask for guidance on how best to keep the coat in good condition (see chapter 14). Grooming also acts as an early warning system, because this is the time when you are most likely to pay close attention to your pup's body.

You also need suitable nail clippers to keep your pup's nails neat and tidy and prevent its feet splaying as a result of overlong nails. Some cotton wool and almond oil is sufficient to clean the ear flaps. Later you may need a pair of scissors to trim excess hair from the dog's feet, and a brush and paste to clean the adult teeth when they come through.

special equipment

You may need to purchase specific equipment if you want to show your pup when it is older. If a lot of grooming is required, it is a good idea to get a grooming table suitable for the adult dog. These tables have non-slip surfaces and help to give the pup confidence.

indoor and outdoor kennels

indoor kennels

An indoor kennel is a great idea for your dog and for you. For the dog, it provides a safe haven, a place of peace and tranquillity where it can sleep in the comfort and security of its own surroundings. Dogs naturally seek out a warm, shaded environment to sleep, and in the wild they would look for a cave or den. To have a place of its own amongst the turmoil of a busy household is bliss for your canine. For you, it gives somewhere where you know the dog is secure while you are not watching it. You know that it cannot come to any harm, nor can it demolish any of your prized possessions while you are unable to give it your full attention.

The indoor kennel can be a home-made enclosure. It should be secure and roomy so that the dog can at the very least lay down flat should it so wish, as well as being able to stand up and turn around. There should be room for a water dish.

Alternatively, and perhaps more conveniently, you can buy a purpose-made crate or cage. These are readily available or can be ordered from most good pet shops. Crates are normally collapsible and so can be transported easily if you go away. In many cases they can be erected in the car for safe travelling (of course, this depends on the size of the car in relation to the cage) or the crate can be folded away when not in use.

When choosing a crate, take into account the fact that your pup will grow and, if possible, buy one that will suit it when it is fully grown. Some vets and dog trainers hire out crates that you can take back or trade in as the pup grows and needs the next size up. There are also available crates originally designed for air travel; these are not collapsible, but if the enclosure is to be kept in one place and does not need to be collapsed for travelling, then they are excellent. You may even be handy enough to make your own!

training the puppy to use a crate

Whether your pup is very young or you are dealing with an older dog, crate training should be an enjoyable experience for dog and trainer alike. At first, the crate will be a strange place to the puppy and, if it is simply thrust in and left, it will be frightened by the strange clanging noises, smells and feeling of being trapped. Therefore, to make sure that the puppy grows to like its new environment, you must take things step by gentle step.

First of all, choose a pleasant spot for the crate, not so much out of the way that the pup cannot see what is going on, but in a quiet corner. Erect it whilst the pup is preoccupied, particularly if it is a little timid, as you will make some noise moving the crate about.

Once it is erected and in place, select a comfortable blanket or two, if possible using some that the pup has already laid on so that the scent is familiar. Leave the gate open and put some treats and perhaps a favourite toy inside. Sit on the floor and encourage the pup to investigate. In many cases the pup will enter the crate, perhaps a little cautiously at first, but it will gain confidence if left and not forced. If after a while the pup shows no signs of wanting to go

indoor and outdoor kennels

Your pup will feel more secure in a busy household if it has a place of its own.

inside, get some choice titbits – freshly cooked chicken or liver – and hold the food through the bars at the back of the cage. If the pup comes around to you ignore it and withdraw the food. As soon as you see it look inside, push some food through the bars and drop a little on to the cage floor. Once the pup realises that it will only get the food by entering the crate, its stomach will lead it there. As it enters the cage, say the keyword that you want it to associate with the action. 'Crate', 'Bed', 'In' – the word does not matter as it is the association that counts. Do not be tempted to rush around and lock the pup in; leave closing the door until it is happy and confident.

An ideal time to train the pup is at mealtimes. It is natural for an animal to take its food to a safe area to eat and, by putting the pup's bowl in the crate, you are helping it to find this safe place. However, once the pup learns that the crate is a good place to be and associates it with your keyword, reduce the amount of food given in the crate to a few titbits, because you could teach the dog to become dominant over its crate by encouraging it to guard its food.

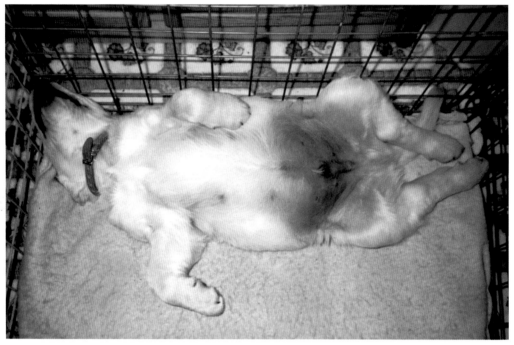

Nine-week-old Golden Retriever Bracken relaxes in his crate.   Photograph by Tony and Ann Bean

Watch your pup's behaviour and you will be able to predict when it is becoming tired. Make sure that it has relieved itself first, as then it is more likely to settle. Entice it into the crate with a chewy treat and, once it is preoccupied, gently close the door. Be ready with another titbit and, if it turns to the door, encourage it back into the body of the crate. If you think it might become distressed or is not ready to settle, open the door whilst it is absorbed by its treat and call it out. Give this a keyword: 'Out', 'Come', or whatever. This puts you in control and not the pup.

It is important to work on teaching the pup to come out of the crate when told as well as to go in; this stops the pup demanding and teaches it to accept your control. There will be times when there is no doubt that it wants to come out, so try to get it to sit or lie down in the crate before it is released, to make sure you maintain your control.

You may well find that your puppy is happier if the crate is covered with a blanket or sheet to make it more private, and more akin to a cave. The secluded atmosphere will give it security and make it more likely to settle. This is also a useful ploy to keep puppies and dogs calm when travelling in a cage. Some dogs become particularly excited by the movement of the car or by watching the world whizz by. Covering the crate will help the dog to keep calm, and prevent anti-social and potentially dangerous behaviours such as barking, whining, and generally hurtling about in the car.

Once the pup is happy to go in the crate, and many will choose to do so if the door is left open, you have a safe place to leave your pup while you are out. The time that the pup is left unattended should be very short to start with, and the pup should have a chew to keep it occupied. See chapter 13 for advice on further training.

indoor and outdoor kennels

outdoor kennels

There are many different views on the ethics of keeping a dog outside in a kennel. Perhaps we should look at the situation from the dog's point of view.

Although the dog has been bred selectively for many hundreds of years, it still maintains many of its basic instinctive behaviours. A number of dogs kept in an indoor environment are driven mad and, indeed, drive their owners mad by the frustration of not being able to do 'doggy' things. For example, it is quite normal to chew, dig, mark territory by urination, to hunt or run to expend energy that in the wild would normally be used for hunting. It is normal to lie with head on paws watching birds, or to chase leaves. If you know that your dog will regularly be left to its own devices, then it is a good idea for the sanity of the dog, yourself and the family to make provisions for the dog to have free access to outdoors.

The traditional idea of a dog chained to a kennel is somewhat outdated and, indeed, defeats the object to quite a large degree. You should choose a much larger and less restricted enclosure or area for the dog. The ideal is a small shed-type kennel which allows the dog to get out of the weather, both hot and cold. The shed should have an entrance large enough for your dog cut into the door, so that the weather has restricted entry. The dog should be able to get out of draughts inside the shed. Provide a bed area within the shed, raised off the floor to prevent dampness. Most dogs like to go up on to a reasonably high bed area. Remember that growing pups should not be encouraged to jump up and down, so start low.

Ideally, the shed should be large enough for you to walk into, which makes it easier to clean. It also helps in the initial training and then later so that you can maintain a dominant position, and/or to attend to the dog if it falls ill.

If your dog lives outdoors, make sure its surroundings are interesting and stimulating.

The shed should be placed on a large concrete or paved area so that the dog can run around as it wishes, and defecate and urinate when it feels the need. Of course, you should provide a large bowl or bucket of fresh water.

You may wish to build a kennel enclosure for your dog from brick or blocks. This is also very acceptable, but tends not to be quite as warm and cosy as a shed. Commercial boarding and breeding kennels cannot be made of wood under the current licensing laws in the United Kingdom, because many different dogs will use the kennel and wood cannot be cleaned as effectively as smooth concrete. The drawback to using wood is the possibility that the dog will chew it. However, if the dog has plenty of stimulus and things to chew, it will be less likely to gnaw the actual fabric of the shed to any serious degree. An important point to remember is that any wood preservative used must be non-toxic.

You may need to consider adding some form of heating, especially for thin-coated dogs or in very cold climates, but a warm and well-insulated bed area with plenty of cosy bedding will be quite adequate, and will encourage your dog to develop a good healthy coat.

Some people may be fortunate in having buildings such as redundant stables that can be converted which, with the addition of an outside run, will allow the dog its freedom.

Give careful thought to the site you choose for the dog. Avoid areas that come into direct contact with any external influences: for instance, don't put your dog's pen next to the fence where children walk past. Children can be wonderful, but they may be inclined to taunt the dog, which will cause behavioural problems that will be difficult for you to deal with. It is best to avoid them if you can. It is also a good idea to choose an area that is sheltered from the elements and provides some cover from the midday sun.

The outdoor area should be as big as you can afford. The bigger and more interesting the dog's enclosure, the less chance there is of the dog getting bored and developing stereotypic, repetitive, compulsive or extreme behaviours. Trees, hardy bushes, platforms for the dog to climb up and lay on, robust safe toys, an upturned dog bed, ropes or old tyres hanging from trees, a hay bale – it is amazing how much pleasure a few simple things can bring to a lonely or bored dog. A barren concrete area may be easier to keep clean, but your dog will not be mentally stimulated, and this is so important, especially while it is young.

You may be able to sacrifice a whole area of the garden to the pup, but you must make sure that it is completely enclosed and safe. Think ahead to the potential jumping power of your dog. Many breeds can easily jump or scale up to 1.8m (6ft) and sometimes even more. Normally, the dog will not jump a high fence unless it can see what is on the other side, but you may have to consider putting a section that angles inwards at the top of the fence or wall to prevent the dog getting over. It is very difficult to train a dog not to jump a fence, particularly if you are not going to be there to reinforce the training. It is safer to put your trust in the enclosure, rather than the dog.

teaching your pup to live outside

The great outdoors can be a daunting place for a very young pup new from the security of its breeder, siblings and mother. Most pups are brought up indoors and, in many cases, will not have seen much of the world. Therefore, to put the pup outside as soon as you get it and leave it there would indeed be very cruel, and have a lasting effect on its future behaviour.

This does not mean that the pup cannot be conditioned quickly to enjoy the outdoor life

indoor and outdoor kennels

and, as long as its needs are taken care of and it is provided with sufficient warmth, it will not be many weeks before the pup is confident in an outdoor enclosure.

It is best to care for the dog indoors for the first few weeks, as its needs are many and the trauma of leaving its litter mates is enough for it to cope with. But time can be spent getting it used to the outdoor enclosure by playing with it and giving some of its meals there. Go out and sit with your pup while it explores and, indeed, have some fun in helping it to discover the things that you have provided to keep it occupied. Shut yourself in the enclosure so that the pup becomes used to the gate being closed. Spend as much time as you can doing this, entering into games and a little training. All the time the dog will be gaining confidence.

A crate is useful when you travel or go away.

Teaching your dog to be left on its own is covered in chapter 13 and the principles of leaving your dog alone in any circumstances are the same: building up time and confidence. You should, however, think about the weather when teaching your pup to be alone outside. A cold pup will be very unhappy, so wait until the weather is pleasant before embarking on this stage. Night time is another stumbling block as the temperature drops and therefore you must be sure that the pup will be warm enough. Also, the night is full of different sounds that can frighten a vulnerable pup, so it is best to wait until it is relatively mature (eight months of age or so), and has learned more about the big outdoors before leaving it alone outside all night.

If the pup is to be living with another dog then often the whole procedure can be speeded up considerably. Assuming that the older animal is confident and social towards it, the pup will, in most cases, follow suit. Even so, it is best to do some ground work before subjecting the pup to being left, and this will also give time for the two to get acquainted and to learn each other's ways.

when puppy comes home

collecting your puppy

It is quite possible that when you bring your pup home this will be its very first trip in a car. Therefore, you need to make sure that the experience is as pleasurable and non-frightening as it can be. If at all possible, take someone with you who can drive while you have the pup on your knee or by your side to reassure it. Take with you:

- a few large towels,
- some newspapers to mop up any accidents,
- a bowl and water for drinking, and
- some bin bags for any soiled materials.

Make sure the breeder knows what time to expect you, as it is best that the pup is not fed just before it travels. Allow plenty of time to let the pup get to know you before you leave. You will need to break a very long journey to allow the pup to empty itself. There is a risk of infection wherever you stop, so choose a place where there are less likely to be lots of dogs and obviously make sure that it is safe from other animals, traffic, and so on.

If necessary, take a snack for yourself and your driver so that you are not tempted to leave the pup for a break. It may be necessary to offer the pup a light meal on a long trip, but if it has shown any signs of travel sickness, such as vomiting or salivating excessively, then stick to water only unless you intend to have a very long break. It won't hurt just this once.

Give the pup a chance to settle in.

getting home

When you first get home take things very gently. Other family members and animals will no doubt be very excited by the new arrival, but try to keep things calm and stop everyone overwhelming the pup. Make sure other animals are out of the way to start with, as you do not want a scuffle on the first meeting. Make sure things are done under your control.

when puppy comes home

When you get home, let your pet out into the garden. Boxer pup photographed by Robert Smith

Probably the first thing the pup will want to do is urinate or defecate, so it is a good idea to put it in the area that you want it to use as a toilet as soon as you get home. If it gets it right this first time, and you are vigilant to its needs from then on, this particular section of training may be easier than you think (see chapter 17).

As your pup starts to find its feet, encourage it to look around the areas where it is to be allowed. There will be areas where it is best the pup does not go. Make sure these areas are blocked from it; do not expect the pup to understand your instructions, but make it impossible for it to go wrong.

Your pup may well feel queasy and, of course, the effect of the change in environment – new smells, sounds and sights – will render it a little disorientated for a while. Do not be surprised if it does not want to eat straight away, even if it is meal time. Just put down some fresh water, and leave your new pet to settle and explore its new environment at its own pace.

When you do offer a meal, make sure that it is food that the pup is used to. There is nothing worse than giving the pup an upset stomach to deal with on top of the trauma of leaving the nest, just because you feel like treating it with a new food or rich titbit.

chapter nine

the first few days

The first few days and nights are the most traumatic period of your pup's young life so far. Up to now, it has had only gentle, gradual changes in its environment, if any, and has had its litter mates and mother to communicate with and to be close to when any unusual or frightening situations arose.

You must take the place of these litter mates and give your puppy care and comfort so that it can develop and grow. In so doing, you will make your own job easier, and you will not be subject to sleepless nights. It is better to keep the pup with you until it learns that it is all right to be alone. At bed time, take it with you for the first few days and make a comfortable, warm area on the floor at the side of your bed. Do not allow the pup on your bed; it will be fine if you offer it your hand in its bed, and comfort it when necessary. Some people prefer to sleep downstairs with the dog until it gets accustomed to its new environment. This works equally well.

Being alone causes the pup anxiety and stress. Essentially it is a pack animal, and company is all it

has known so far. When stressed, the pup will be more inclined to do what we perceive as anti-social things such as howling, barking, chewing, and emptying the contents of its stomach and bladder. Patience and understanding in these early stages will help avoid problems in the future.

introducing other animals

Be careful how you introduce the pup to other animals. It is often best to sit or kneel down with the pup on your lap, and let the other animals come to inspect the new arrival. Speak calmly and quietly to all of them, and maintain your own position of control. Most other animals will recognise the pup as a young animal and not see it as a threat. As the pup gains in confidence, it may take liberties with other pets so do not be surprised if it gets chastised by them. If this happens, do not go running to the pup's defence. Of course you cannot allow a

when puppy comes home

potentially dangerous situation, but on the other hand the pup needs to learn its place and older animals, especially older dogs, in most cases will teach this with a low growl or occasional snap. If the situation appears to be getting a little heated, step in and make both animals do something for you, thus enforcing your own position over them.

As a general rule, always pet, reward and feed the older animal first. Observe the hierarchy within your pack and give your attention to the most dominant animal first, and then *pro rata* down the line. By so doing, you are leaving the other animals in no doubt about who is most dominant and then, as long as you maintain your position above the top dog, you should have a relatively peaceful household.

Offer food that the pup is used to. Photograph by Miss T Chadwick

Let the resident animal come to investigate the newcomer.

nutrition, feeding
and behaviour

Giving the correct and suitable diet is a very important aspect of bringing up a pup. The diet has a direct bearing on both its physical development and behaviour. In this instance, I refer not so much to what many call 'abnormal' behaviour, as this is the context normally linked to nutrition, but to the understanding of normal canine behaviour.

feeding the best

Many puppy owners think that they know better than the breeder and even ignore the vet's advice. Many tend to overdo everything that they are told, thinking that if a little is good, more must be even better! One of the most common bad practices is overfeeding calcium and other additives. We all know that a growing animal needs calcium for developing bones, but too much can be as bad as not enough.

So how do you get the correct nutrition into your pup without becoming neurotic about its diet? By far the easiest way is to purchase a good-quality, ready-prepared diet, taking care that the product you buy is specifically designed for your pup's age or, as it is now more commonly termed, 'lifestage'. There are many good foods on the market that cater for all your pup's needs, without the necessity for additives of any kind.

If you have bought the pup from a breeder who recommends a particular regime, and if you are happy that the pup you have purchased is fit, well, and of a good weight when you collect it, then there is no valid reason to change the diet. It makes sense to stay with the product while it matches the pup's growth stage. Later, you may have to change or, providing you are getting good results, go on to the next 'lifestage' in the same brand. All major brands are available at many outlets and, even though you may have to order the food from smaller shops, it is worth doing so to maintain your puppy's good health and development.

It does not always follow that the most expensive food is the best, but it pays to be choosy and disregard any foods that would be difficult for the pup to digest, or are not specifically designed for its age. The best food for your pup does not have to cost the earth, but in general the better quality foods have a higher percentage of digestibility, which means that more of what goes into the pup stays in its system for it to utilise.

The faeces should be firm and not over-abundant under normal circumstances. However, it is not unusual for the pup to be a little 'loose' when it is under stress or over-excited, so it makes sense to give it a few days to settle into its new home before deciding to change the food that the breeder has successfully used so far. Observe the litter of pups before you bring yours away and, if possible, watch your own pup producing stools before you separate it from the litter. If the faeces are firm, then it is unlikely that the breeder's choice of food is the cause of stomach upsets and runny stools.

Naturally, if the pup has diarrhoea or any other form of upset, then action must be taken very quickly to prevent dehydration, and a veterinary opinion should be sought. You should tell the vet whether or not the stools of your pup and its litter mates were all right, otherwise the vet may decide that the pup needs a change of diet when it is not really necessary.

It is a good idea to give a very young pup a milky meal made from a proprietary brand of bitch milk substitute or goat's milk. It is best not to use cow's milk as it gives the pup little nutritional benefit. Puppies relish this type of meal and often accept it in preference to a heavier meal if they are off colour, under stress or not too hungry.

home-made diets

If you have a lot of spare time you may wish to provide your dog with a fresh, home-made diet, and there are many books providing information on just how to go about this. It is essential to be very aware of all the nutrients necessary so that your dog has a good balanced diet, and it takes a very dedicated person to get this right all the time. For most people, time is better spent training, guiding and teaching the pup the house rules as well as having fun together, building a relationship, and finding things to do that they can share.

Do not allow your puppy to guard its bowl.

detecting poisons

Although we have taken away from dogs the need to hunt and develop food-finding skills, in many cases they still retain some of the finer skills, such as the ability to assess the safety of suitable food. However, I have known a dog that regularly picked up small amounts of rat poison (Waferin) by eating treated grain put out to control vermin. His owner noticed a deterioration in the dog's health and consulted the vet over a slight cough, but the misdemeanour was not detected until the dog's system reached overload point, coupled with the slight stress of being put into a boarding kennels. He started to spout blood from every orifice but his life was saved by prompt action from the kennel staff and the vet giving a Vitamin K injection.

Puppies in particular are very inquisitive and, just like human babies, test most things in their mouths. You must therefore be very vigilant about what the puppy has access to, including poisonous garden plants, toxic paints, pesticides, and so on.

loss of appetite

It is common for a pup not to want to eat when it has suffered the change of environment and routine associated with going to a new home. It feels disorientated and distressed and, if after a couple of meal times have elapsed and it is still not eating, you might have to feed it a tasty morsel or two by hand to 'kick start' it into eating again. The same might apply the first time you take it away from home. The only danger is that, if you continue hand feeding, this then becomes an attention-seeking behaviour and the pup refuses to eat except when hand fed. If this happens, make sure that your pup gets plenty of attention at other times, and put a little food down on the floor for it to eat. You may have to harden your heart if it does not eat straight away, but as soon as it does eat, reward it with praise and put another tasty morsel into its dish. Healthy dogs do not deliberately starve themselves in the presence of good food. Be patient. If the dog does not eat, take up the food and try again later.

If a pup is travel sick during its journey home, it may refuse to eat the food that it has been used to, because it associates the taste of the food with being ill. The pup reacts just as we might under the same circumstances; we are often loath to eat that meal again, and certainly do not want it the next day. Sometimes this aversion goes on for a long time.

In order to keep the dog to the chosen diet you must gradually build back to it by feeding a light meal of something else – scrambled eggs, white fish, chicken, strong-flavoured fish such as sardines or pilchards, or a well-processed 'human style' cereal such as wheat flakes. Even a little fishy cat food can tempt a choosy animal. Over a few days gradually return to the original diet by mixing ever-increasing amounts of the correct food into the pup's meals. If the pup is still reluctant to eat, mix in a small amount of vegetable or fish oils, meat stock, fat, or a spoonful of fresh mince or tinned puppy meat to tempt the pup, but aim to get back to the correct balance as soon as possible.

It is not unusual for a pup to refuse some meals, and it is important not to panic when this happens. In the wild it is normal for adult dogs not to eat every day although, of course, pups must eat more regularly, and the mother would try to ensure a reasonably regular supply of food. But this supply would not be tuned to the clock as it tends to be in many domestic households. If your pup misses a meal, simply pick up the food and feed it at the next meal time. If you are feeding to need, that is, allowing the pup to eat as much as it wants at each meal, it will undoubtedly reach a point where it needs a rest. As long as it is drinking and showing no signs of ill health, let it be the judge of when it needs the next meal. If it goes more than 24 hours, and is not tempted even by choice titbits, or if it shows any other signs of ill health, then look for other reasons for the lack of appetite and seek veterinary advice.

In most cases owners assume that the pup needs more food than it really does, and are concerned when the lovingly-prepared meal is rejected. Dogs do not possess our scruples, and will not eat to make *you* feel better!

nutrition, feeding *and behaviour*

If your pups' tummies are upset, offer a meal such as scrambled egg.

It is more common for smaller breeds to refuse to eat than it is for larger animals. This is to be expected because evolution has played a part in giving the larger animal a pre-disposition to eat readily and opportunistically to satisfy its greater needs.

Some animals refuse to eat because they have an allergy to something in the com-mercially-prepared diet (often gluten). After eating certain foods they may feel ill, and therefore refuse them in future. We do not know this, and may feel that they are being awkward when in fact they are being quite sensible.

It is not uncommon for low-ranking animals to be reluctant to feed until they are sure that others have finished. In a household where there are several animals, all the animals must be fully aware that the human is the one in control and not one of the other animals. Obviously there will be a structure of hierarchy amongst the animals but you must remain above them all to maintain discipline in the ranks. Feed the animals in order of position in the pack so that they do not become confused or feel the need to boost their position in the pack.

You should not fall into the trap of allowing the pup to dictate meal times by giving in to its demands for food, particularly at times when you would not normally be feeding. This sort of behaviour can lead to dominance very quickly, and can become a real problem.

chapter *ten*

teaching good behaviour at mealtimes

The pup's mealtimes It is important that the pup understands that humans are the providers of food and so must be respected and not challenged. Once your pup has had a few days to settle in, then teach it that there is no threat when humans or other animals go near its food.

Mealtimes also provide good opportunities to condition your dog's behaviour. *Always* ask it to do something for you before you put down its food. Within a few days of getting your pup, start to teach it the meaning of simple keywords such as 'sit' (see chapter 17). Use this at meal times and maintain control all the time. Allow yourself time to follow through this training; feeding time should not be a matter simply of putting down the food and walking away leaving the dog to eat in peace. Feeding is an important social activity, and if the dog is left to its own devices it is far more likely to develop behavioural problems. Start as you mean to go on and feed your dog out in the open. Do not allow it to guard its food in a secluded corner, in another room or outside, unless you are with it.

Step one: Prepare the pup's food, but keep a few tasty titbits to one side. Put down the bowl and then, as the dog starts to relish its contents, bend down, put your hand towards the bowl and allow the pup to take the titbits from your hand, or drop them into the dish. The pup learns that you being near its food has benefits, rather than is something to be wary of.

Step two: At the next meal, sit down on the floor with the dog's bowl and feed the pup from your hand a piece at a time, which reinforces the message that you are in control. Introduce a control key word, 'Eat', that means the dog can eat.

Step three: At the next meal, put the bowl on the floor, but half way through the meal take it up, and let the dog watch you put in more tasty titbits. Hold the bowl up above its head until it goes into the sit position. Tell it, 'Sit', and then, 'Eat' and give back the food.

Step four: At the next meal, sit holding the bowl. Tell the pup to 'Sit' and then 'Eat'. While the dog eats, keep putting your hand in the bowl and stirring the contents, offering it a mouthful from your hand, and then withdrawing your hand.

Step five: At the next meal, put only half the food in the bowl. Tell the pup 'Sit' and then 'Eat', allow it to eat from the bowl on the floor, pick up the bowl, say 'Sit', add the rest of the food and then hold the bowl while you tell the pup to eat. Keep hold of the bowl until it finishes.

If at *any* time during feeding the dog shows *any* sign of growling, you must take the food away, and then feed a little piece at a time from your hand. Once you are confident with this and there is no more growling, feed the pup from a small dish which you refill continually from a main dish which stays out of the dog's reach. Keep using the control words 'Sit' and 'Eat'.

If you are foolhardy enough to dismiss a growl as 'puppy feeling his feet', the problem will develop and it won't be long before everyone has to be warned not to go near the dog while it is feeding. This human solution compounds the problem, and reinforces in the dog's mind that it has control over food. If this situation gets out of hand, other problems can then multiply. If you want to keep your dog, maintain control – now!

Next get other adult members of the family to follow this same procedure and, when you are sure the dog is happy to accept their interference, help the children to do the same under your supervision. Encourage even very young children by standing behind them and offering your assistance and back-up all the time. Make sure the procedure is carried out correctly, guiding the child's hand with your own if necessary to prevent anything going wrong.

Once the dog is aware that every human has control, it will be easier to deal with in all respects. Controlling food is a very important part of the whole control of the dog.

Human mealtimes There is no doubt that the smells emanating from the kitchen and table are very tempting even to the human nose. Therefore it is not unreasonable for the dog, with its superior 'nose power', to be excited by the smells. It is also natural to take pity on the owner of those forlorn eyes that are glued to every mouthful you are eating. Dogs soon learn who is the 'soft touch' who eventually will slip them a choice titbit.

Begging at the table can become a real problem in some households, and usually becomes so because the humans respond to the dog's demands. Sometimes the dog is actually minding its own business when it is actively encouraged to come to the table, and at other times children tempt the dog by dropping food – accidentally or on purpose. It is amazing what some dogs will eat from the table that they would turn up their noses at if offered as a meal in their dog dish!

It is best to set strict rules and make sure that the whole family is aware of and abides by them. If the family cannot be trusted, it is better to put the dog outside, in another room, or on a lead so that it can be physically controlled until it understands more commands and obeys your voice. Once it understands the key word for 'Down' or 'Bed', then it can be kept in a down position, or sent to its bed area or crate while you eat.

It is important that the pup understands that humans have priority where food is concerned, particularly with those breeds and characters likely to err on the dominant side. Therefore, feed yourself and other family members before you feed the pup. I know this is not always practical, but it is important that the dog feels that this is the case. Have a light snack or pretend to eat before the dog, and it will get the idea.

how many meals?

New puppy owners are often in a quandary as to how many meals the young pup should consume, knowing that it needs at least four meals a day at six to eight weeks of age. At what point should this be reduced? The best method is to be guided by the pup. You will find that it will fairly quickly reduce to three meals a day itself, by simply refusing or picking at one of the meals. When this happens, simply drop that meal. By the age of 12 weeks most puppies will have weaned themselves down to three meals. After this, the size of breed and development rate has a bearing on the number of meals required and the rate at which this reduces, but again be guided by the dog's weight, condition, appetite and willingness to eat each meal.

chapter *ten*

how much should you feed?

The best practice is to allow the pup to eat its fill at each meal, and then remove any leftovers. Avoid feeding after the pup has been very active; first let it rest before offering food.

If the pup is not overweight, allow it to regulate the food intake itself. If it starts to put on too much weight, reduce the amount given at one of the meals. Watch its shape and feed to maintain the dog in good condition, rather than following a rule book. Amounts of food suggested on the side of dog food sacks and tins are only guidelines. Every dog is different; some eat a lot and do not put on weight, others require far less. Good condition shows in the whole of the dog: its coat, activity levels, eyes. Learn to observe and monitor little changes, as this is the best form of preventative medicine. It is not healthy for a pup to carry too much weight as this puts strain on the limbs and, indeed, the whole system.

If your puppy is eating well and is underweight, there could be some reason why it is not maintaining its weight. It is best to pay an early visit to the veterinary surgeon if you are concerned, rather than trying to solve the mystery yourself.

eating the wrong things

In the strange new world to which you have brought your puppy there are many weird and wonderful things to see, hear, smell, touch and taste. Touch and taste are very close to each other for a pup. Because it is not a very dextrous animal, most of its tactile ability is confined to its mouth, so many items find their way there, not all of them suitable. In most cases the puppy will identify what should and should not be eaten by trial and error, but sometimes its perception of a good chew is not shared by the humans of the family!

Most puppies obey their natural instincts and do not ingest dangerous items, but modern man-made packages and other objects with strange and interesting textures and smells can sometimes tempt the pup to eat something that might do it harm. In most cases, indigestible materials pass through the animal with relative ease, but it makes sense to try to prevent and avoid such things, just in case the pup eats something that could cause some damage. This means being as vigilant for the pup as you would be for a human toddler. It is good practice to leave out only those items that cannot damage the dog, or are specifically designed for it. Also, early teaching of the meaning of the key word 'Leave' is of paramount importance to maintain control of the dog's consumption when out and about (see chapter 17).

eating faeces

The consuming of faeces (coprophagy), is one of the most distasteful things that a pup can do, at least as far as its human companions are concerned. As far as the pup is concerned, there is nothing wrong with this behaviour and it is perfectly normal.

There are various reasons why this behaviour starts. It is possible that the diet does not have the correct balance. Lack of trace elements or diets high in carbohydrates and starch may be the factors that arouse the behaviour in the dog.

It is normal for a bitch to clean up her puppies' stools, and it is also normal for dogs to be tempted by the smell of rotting or decaying meat. For whatever reason, once a dog tries eating the act becomes self-rewarding, because it tastes good! The stools do not even have to be the dog's own; they can be the droppings of sheep, horses, cows, other dogs, cats — even human effluence is not objected to. Some pups simply grow out of the behaviour, and it is certainly more common in young animals. There are various ways of dealing with the problem:

Step one: First make sure that the dog has a good quality diet suitable for its age and needs.

Step two: Give the meals at more regular intervals, and allow the pup to eat its fill to make sure it is gaining sufficient bulk and nutrients from the diet.

Step three: Be ultra clean by teaching the dog to go to toilet on command (see chapter 17), and always clean up after it.

Each puppy has to find its position in the hierarchy, but humans must come top. Photo by P Richards

Step four: Never leave the pup free in an area where there are any stools.

These simple steps may be sufficient to deal with the problem but, if it continues, treat the stools by coating them with a distasteful, yet harmless, substance such as Epsom Salts or red pepper. Allow the dog to sniff and taste them, and it will then find them far less attractive. You will have to set this up a few times to break the habit. It is possible to put additives into the dog's diet that, once they have gone through the dog, make the stools taste unpleasant and thus discourage the dog from eating them. Obviously you should not give these substances for very long, but a seven-day course of a small dose of ferrous sulphate will do the trick. Check with your vet to make sure it is safe and for the correct dosage for your animal. There are other products on the market that also act as a preventative, and your vet will advise you on these.

learning through play

The puppy learns a tremendous amount through play. In the wild, play helps it to perfect its hunting skills, but in a domestic dog is does not have to hunt for its own food. You can, however, use the desire to play to your advantage as a motivator to help you train the dog. Indeed, if you do not harness this basic urge, the dog can become very boisterous and may cause problems. We keep our dogs permanently at juvenile level, and it is important that their behaviour never develops to such a degree that they feel that they are at the top of the pack.

controlling games

The playing and, more importantly, the winning of games is one of the contributory factors that help to determine position in the hierarchy. The pack structure is much more subtle than the leaders always being the winners and the losers the underlings. However, it is important that the top dog instigates the games, wins and takes possession of the toys.

It is important that you do have toys for your puppy, but make sure that the toys are yours and the pup knows they are yours. It should be allowed to play with them only on your terms.

Pups like to play...   Photograph by Liz Phillips

If you have chosen a breed of dog more prone to dominant tendencies, it is particularly important to make sure that the dog does not have free access to toys. The vast majority of dogs referred to behavioural consultants because of dominance have free access to toys and, in many cases, a toy box of their own. The dog should not be allowed to thrust toys at you and demand play. It is acceptable for you to send the dog for a toy and then sit in a chair playing catch, but be careful if the dog is demanding to play, or it may construe your agreement to play as a step up the ladder to the top. You will be amused the first time it scratches, barks or grunts to catch your attention, but if you give in to the dog's demands each time, it will soon start to manipulate you. When you do not respond, you may be rewarded by a nip from your dog, which by now assumes that it can get you to play on *its* command.

Tug games are a good way of building

a rapport with your dog but, again, if the dog is allowed to win and run off with its prize, you could be paving the way to dominance over possessions. Another problem can occur if the dog's toys are scattered around for it to play with at will, even if it has not become dominant over them. When you want to use those toys as motivators in your training, and particularly if you want to train a specific exercise or train out a particular problem, you will not be able to use them effectively because the dog will be bored with them and look to other things to play with. If you carry a favourite squeaky toy on a walk and bring it out when you want the dog to come to you, this works very well if the toy has not been seen for a while. However, if the dog has had access to the toy whenever it wants at home, it is more likely to take one look and say, 'So what! I'd rather sniff this tree!'

... so use this to your advantage when training your pup.

the benefits of play

Play is a great motivator, and many trainers of top-level obedience and working dogs use toys and play as motivation and encouragement. Play can be used as a link between the known and the unknown, and can help the dog overcome its fears. Having a game when a potentially frightening situation is developing can help the dog to relax and learn that its fears are not justified, or at least can be dealt with.

Toys that can be held by both dog and handler are particularly useful in manipulating the dog into certain positions. Once the dog's attention is focussed on the toy, the handler can put it away a pocket. The dog will maintain its attention on the handler, and can be encouraged away from distractions at the merest squeak or rustle.

Unlike food, toys and games do not run out. Food is easily dropped, and the dog can end up with its nose on the floor sniffing out fallen titbits instead of concentrating on the job in hand. It is easy to run out of food or to sicken the dog by using too much and, of course, there is the added problem of your dog's waist-line to consider!

Many trainers use a combination of food and play to motivate their dog, particularly when teaching something new or which has a degree of difficulty, and this is perhaps the best strategy.

social *training*

the first few weeks

When you first get your puppy probably it will be about seven or eight weeks old. It will not be fully inoculated, and therefore is at risk if you allow it in areas where other dogs go that may have not been inoculated themselves. It will also be in need of much emotional and physical support and guidance from you.

A caring breeder will have inoculated the pup's mother before she became pregnant and she will have passed on some of this immunity to her offspring. However, most vets advise that, whatever the background of the pup, you should not take it out until it is fully inoculated, and allow a couple of weeks after this to be on the safe side. Unfortunately, this timing coincides with the most important few weeks of the pup's life with you, and it needs to have as many stimulating and worldly experiences as possible in order to develop and become a normal, intelligent and well-adjusted dog. Puppies deprived of sufficient stimulation and sheltered from the real world develop abnormal and often extreme behaviours, making it difficult for you to integrate them into a normal lifestyle.

Therefore, you must look for ways of protecting the dog's physical and mental health. There are many things that you can do and situations you can introduce to the pup, keeping disease risk to a minimum.

puppy parties and play groups

Many forward-thinking vets now organise puppy parties or play groups which bring together families and their puppies to help with social skills, to advise on the behavioural aspects of the pup's well-being and on basic health care. They are sometimes run by the vet or veterinary nurse, or a behavioural trainer is invited to take the class; sometimes it is a combination of the two. These gatherings should be constructive – the puppies are allowed a certain amount of freedom but not to have a free-for-all!

the great outdoors!

While your pup is small enough to carry, take it into the big outdoors without its feet coming into contact with contaminated pathways and roads. It will learn much from the safety of your protective arm, and will understand which noises, smells and sights are not to be feared.

social training

You can take the pup visiting to households without dogs or where you know the dogs are 'pup friendly', fully inoculated, and not allowed to go into high disease-risk areas. Your pup needs to learn about humans that do not live in your household, so invite children and older people to visit and allow controlled interaction. Do not shelter the pup from appliances such

as hairdryers and vacuum cleaners. Good breeders will have introduced these things already, but your machines might sound different to the pup. Try to get someone else to do the vacuum cleaning to start with, while you hold the pup and give it confidence. (What a good excuse to get out of housework: 'Sorry, I'm training the puppy'!)

Things that the pup has not seen before will often make it nervous. Place all kinds of different objects in the garden or kitchen so that the pup can investigate and learn at its own pace. Find lots of things for the pup to do. Encourage it to explore, search for hidden handkerchiefs or toys, teach it simple exercises and even a few tricks. The more you stimulate its senses and brain, the more adaptable, well adjusted and easy to train it will be.

Siberian Husky Remus settles in. Photograph by K Butler

travelling in the car

Before your pup is inoculated, you can take your pup out in the car as much as you like. The majority of puppies nowadays come to their new home by car, and in most cases they travel well, especially if you do not feed them immediately before a journey, and give them the security of a human to reassure them. It is best if the pup travels in the back of the car and, eventually, you will want it behind a dog guard or in a crate for security. If the pup is in the front, it should be on the floor in the well and not on the seat by the driver, as this is very distracting, potentially dangerous and, in some countries, illegal.

A tail gate in your car is most useful.

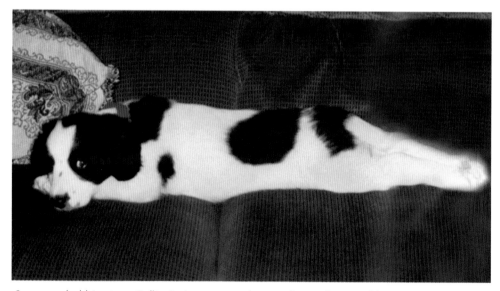

Seven-week-old Jamie, a Collie–Springer cross, does not know about muddy paws.
Photograph by Tina Wilson

You can start by training the pup to travel on the back seat with a human, but eventually it will have to be taught to travel in the back. This can be done by teaching good associations with the back of the car, and with being on its own.

Step one: Feed the pup in the back when the car is stationary. Sit beside it with the back door open. Stroke it and keep it calm.

Step two: Teach the pup to lie down in the back by doing the 'Down' exercise described in chapter 17.

Step three: Get the dog used to the door being shut by gently closing it for a few seconds and then opening it and rewarding the dog calmly. Slowly increase the time the door is shut and give the pup something to occupy itself with, such as a chew or titbit.

Step four: When you are confident that the pup is settled, start the engine but do not move off. Return to the back and make sure the pup is happy, and repeat the above stages with the engine running.

Step five: When the pup is confident with steps one to four, drive a very short distance. If it has shown no signs of travel sickness on previous journeys you can give it a chew stick to keep it occupied.

Soon the pup will travel happily in the back on its own. By now you will be well on with the training of the essential control exercises so you will be able to use your keyword for 'Down' to keep the pup under control.

If you do not have an estate or hatchback car, then a doggy travel harness might be a good investment. This helps secure the dog to the seat belt, giving it safety and preventing it from wandering around. Alternatively a crate may fit on the back seat and create a secure environment for the pup.

The more journeys the pup takes, the more it will come to understand and enjoy the experience, and many well-trained pups try to get into the car rather than avoid it.

It is safest and best for the pup to lie down while the car is moving. A pup automatically lies down on the first journey as this is a

You can take your pup into many environments as long as you carry it to help avoid direct contact with disease.   Photograph by G Lewis

submissive position and it does not wish to antagonise anyone in a situation that it is unsure of. Later it might try to stand up, but you should keep it in a down position as this also helps to avoid travel sickness. Travel sickness is often caused by the dog watching the movement out of the window. Excitable or anxious dogs become more agitated if they are allowed to stand and watch, so gently and calmly persevere and keep the pup to the down position if it is at all possible. You will find it easier if you have a friend to drive, as this allows you more time to concentrate on the pup.

Excitable and/or obsessive breeds, such as the Border Collie, can become very 'hyped up' in the car. At worst, they become aggressive, biting at the furniture and seat belts, and even your hand; at best, there is obsessive barking, whining and trying to 'catch' passing cars through the window. This is not good for the dog, the car or the concentration of the driver. You can avoid this behaviour by training correctly and not allowing the dog to move around freely. If you are on your own, you need to find some way of restricting the pup's movement. A travelling box or crate is ideal for this and gives the pup added security. A good tip is to cover the crate with a white sheet; this keeps it cool by reflecting the sun and stops the pup getting excited by observing the movement.

Who is sharing with whom?

setting the rules

Even before your puppy comes home you should have made certain decisions as to what rules are to be observed by both it and the rest of the family.

All households have rules, some to do with the social structure and some more practical. Simple conditions, such as not coming into the lounge with muddy boots, not leaving a dirty bath, or always letting the rest of the family know when you might be late are all rules that humans accept because it makes day-to-day living with the rest of the family much easier.

A dog may come into a household and run riot because no rules have been set for it to follow. The difficulty with dogs is that they do not think in the same way that we do. For instance, if a child comes into the house with muddy boots, we can point out the error of his ways, explain about the mess and the difficulty of keeping the house clean, and the child will understand – at least to a degree.

The dog, on the other hand, cannot understand the concept of 'muddy'. After it runs in

from the garden with dirty paws and you try to explain the error of its ways, it is at a loss to understand a word. Yes, it may understand that you are not pleased from your tone, body language and attitude, but why? It has no idea.

access in the house

There are common problems that occur when dogs are allowed free access to all areas of the house. Apart from possible damage, there is the issue of dominance. If you have no areas that are exclusive to humans, the dog may decide that it is on a par with all the humans in the hierarchy. Should you want it out of the way at any time, it may challenge your authority in the only way it knows, by growling or, worse still, biting. Therefore it is best to make rules from the start. Decide on areas where it is acceptable for the dog to go at any time, or that can be blocked if the need arises. Close doors to areas of importance. For instance, my dogs are allowed in the kitchen and hallway from the garden while I am present, because these areas are easily cleaned and there is little chance of damage. All other areas have their doors closed and the dogs cannot gain free access. They can, however, come into those other rooms on my invitation.

If at all possible, it is a good idea for your dog to have a reasonably-sized area in which it can be enclosed if you are out of the house or when you are very busy. If you will be out for long periods at a time, even if this is only occasionally, then an outside area is essential. If you leave it only for short periods, then an indoor kennel will suffice (see chapter 8). By creating a safe area you are doing yourself and the dog a favour. The dog will appreciate a place of its own where it is safe, and you will not come home to chewed-up furniture or mess in the house.

Bedrooms are another cause of contention. A dominant dog should not be allowed in the bedroom and, more particularly, never on the bed. If you wish to remain at the top of the pack, you must maintain your own bed area and not allow the dog to share or, worse still, have free access to it. If you want to have your dog in the bedroom, take it with you when you go to the bedroom and make it wait outside the room when you go to the bathroom. When you enter the bedroom, call it in and make it lie by the side of the bed on the floor or on its own

Mungo is only relaxing – but what is he learning?

bed at floor level. If it shows any sign of growling or dominant body stance, immediately stop this privilege. If you allow anything more, even the smallest and sweetest of dogs may get 'ideas above its station'; you could end up with problems that are very difficult for you to deal with and may result in you having to get rid of the dog. It is most disturbing to have the once pleasant face of your pet growling and snarling while you lie in bed, and it will be your own doing if you do not set the rules now – and stick to them! You may think that this will not happen to you and that your sweet little puppy will never be like that. Many new owners feel this way and ignore advice, but six months to a year later are extremely upset by their dog's apparently abnormal, but in reality quite normal, behaviour.

feeding time

Feeding and table manners also need their own set of rules. Start as you mean to go on; do not allow the pup to scrounge from the table or, for that matter, allow humans to throw titbits to the pup. Feed the pup only from its own dishes and in an open area so that it is difficult for it to guard its food, do not always feed in exactly the same spot, and always make the pup do something, such as 'Sit', or 'Down', before it is fed.

Feeding time is an ideal time to practise training techniques, because you will have the pup's full attention and it will be very keen to please. This also gives you a much greater level of mental control over the dog, and it will be less likely to challenge your authority when it knows you control its food to a high degree.

social training

furniture

Whether or not to let the pup on the furniture is another dilemma. The pup will not know when it has dirty paws, and, again, the dominance rule applies: an elevated position is a position of power. Therefore, teach the dog to come on to the furniture only when invited (chapter 17).

doorways

It is important that dogs do not barge through doors as, even if you are reasonably strong, the results can be disastrous if you are carrying something and the dog pushes by. And again, remember the dominance rule. The leader of the pack goes through gaps first to investigate the other side. This must be you. (See chapter 17.)

biting or mouthing

Most puppies bite or mouth your hand, especially when they are very young and going through the teething period. This can be very painful as their teeth are needle sharp. Biting and mouthing is a very natural behaviour for a dog and therefore a certain amount of

mouthing and chewing is necessary. The dog finds out about its environment with its mouth, and learns just how hard it should or should not bite. But you must draw the line somewhere. The best way to control this is to allow the dog to start a little mouthing on your arm but, when it begins to get a little too excited, withdraw immediately and say 'No'. Show that you are hurt and that you no longer want to play – ignore its attentions. Once it has backed off, invite it to play; this time introduce a play rag or tugger toy. Encourage it to bite this, but if it catches your skin, immediately withdraw and stop the game. Again show by your attitude and body language that you are hurt and you no longer want to play.

Most puppies want to play, and therefore very soon learn to play on your terms. Children are very good at this exercise because their skin is more tender and they tolerate fewer bites before withdrawing. Do not put young children at risk of getting hurt; train the dog yourself first.

Many people are tempted to tap the dog's nose or smack it when it bites. In

Teach your puppy the extent to which it can bite or mouth.

most cases the dog does not respond in the desired manner. It thinks that this is all part of the game; you are playing rough so it joins in the fun and plays rough too. If you can shout, it can bark or growl, which increases its excitement. You must remember that the puppy is simply playing puppy games and, unless you teach it your rules in a way that it can understand, it will use its own set of rules. Observe puppies in a litter playing with their siblings — they play rough. Only when they go too far do the litter mates walk away and say 'enough is enough'.

toys

It is good for puppies to have safe toys, and they can serve as great training aids. However, there is a danger that the puppy will start to rule your life with its toys. At first, this is very subtle and you will not notice it happening. You encourage the puppy to play and it discovers that, if it brings the toys to you, you will play with it. Sounds cute, doesn't it? Either you or the pup may decide on a special area where the toys are to be kept, a toy box or even its bed, and you tidy up after it, collecting all the toys and putting them together. Some dogs start to become possessive over these toys, and you may hear the odd growl or notice a subtly-dominant body posture taken over them. When you ignore this, the pup interprets it as a victory, and so takes another step up the ladder of 'Who's Boss'. Left to progress, this behaviour is potentially dangerous, and someone will end up by getting bitten. This will probably mean that the dog has to be re-homed and the problem passed on to someone else or, worse still, destroyed.

The correct way to play with toys is for you to maintain the control of them. If you play games with the pup, you must win. You must end up with ultimate possession of the toy. Avoid entering into games that you may not win. At the end of the game (and you decide when the end will be, don't wait for the dog to tire), put the toys away out of the pup's reach.

The pup should not run off with its toy.   Photograph by Maria Carter

The toys are *your* toys, and the pup is allowed to play with them at *your* discretion. You might feel that the pup should win some games, but if you want to maintain mental and physical control, you are well advised to heed this advice. The pup will win many other advantages through its life that you will not even be aware of, so whenever you can do something actively to lower its position in the hierarchy with the humans, you must do so.

Another advantage of this regime is that the toys then become a wonderful training aid. Because the pup does not have free access to the toys they are interesting and are associated with having fun with you. That is a great basis for working on your relationship with the pup.

Put a special toy in your pocket when you go out for a walk. Either as part of the training, or when you want the dog to return, bring out the toy (especially if it has a squeak), and the dog will be keen to come back and play with you. If you call the pup and it sees this as the end of its fun, it is far less likely to want to come back, and this is the start of one of the most common behavioural problems: 'My dog won't come back when he is called'. Start as you mean to go on and you will never have this problem.

Get to know your pup.

Pups can be taught all sorts of tricks with toys. You can exercise great control by teaching the dog to put things away under command. It will not see this as 'tidying up' but as something interesting and fun to do.

going to the vet

Probably one of the first visits your pup will experience is to the veterinary surgeon for a check up, and perhaps its first inoculation. This can be a traumatic time, but it does not need to be so. Unless you are worried about some aspect of your pup's health, allow it a couple of days to settle in and to build up its confidence in you.

chapter *twelve*

A pup that has been well socialised by the breeder will be relatively confident in new situations, and even if it is a little unsure you can play a big part in making the visit as pleasant as possible. Practise putting the pup on a table at home, because this is what will happen at the surgery. Hold it safely against your body, put your arm around it and reassure it and, as it starts to settle, give a reward. Do this two or three times a day. Give a keyword, such as 'Table', to associate with the new lesson. Soon the pup will be quite happy with this new experience, and it will be one less thing for it to try to comprehend when it goes to the surgery. Once the pup is becoming confident, try to bring it into the stand position.

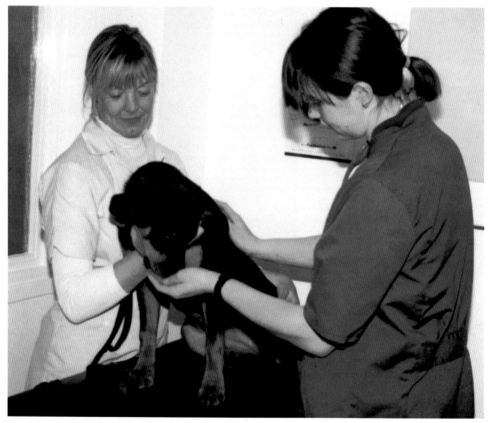

The pup's visit to the vet should be as pleasant as possible.

When the day comes for the visit, try to arrange a quiet time for your appointment so that there are not too many other dogs around. Write down any questions you may have, as it is easy to forget what you have to say when you get into the surgery. Go armed with some treats for your pup. Do not put your pup on the floor in the waiting room, as many sick animals will have been there and the risk of infection is high even in the cleanest of places. If your pup is too large to carry and hold on your lap, leave it in the car with a friend, or ask the receptionist to call you when it is your turn to go in.

When you enter the surgery the vet will ask you to place the pup on the table. Do just as you did at home and keep a supportive arm around your pup. Offer it a treat and, even if it does not take it, the sight and smell will be familiar and help it to relax. A good vet will take time to say 'Hello' to the pup and build its confidence before he checks it over. He may even have his own supply of treats. Talk to the pup soothingly all the time. The vet may want to take the pup's temperature, which means that he will insert a thermometer into the pup's anus. The pup probably will not worry about this too much, but will need to be standing, so once again your training comes into its own. Other tests may include testing the heart rate, checking ears, mouth, eyes and feeling the abdomen. Then comes the inoculation. Hold the pup as directed by the vet, normally sideways on but with its head facing you. Soothe it with your voice, stroking it all the while. The vet will inoculate into the very loose skin between the back of the neck and the pup's shoulders. With any luck, the pup won't even notice. Reward it again, and ask the vet to fuss it, especially if the pup did feel the needle. It is important that the pup is not unduly frightened by the experience, so take as much time as the vet will allow.

Most puppies come out from their first visit to the veterinary surgeon with a clean bill of health. Listen carefully to what you are told and, if in doubt, ask for an explanation. Do not be afraid to discuss any problems – remember that you are paying for this. If you have not been given worming tablets for the pup from your breeder, get some from the vet. They will be suitable and effective, and take away any uncertainty you may have if buying them over the counter at a pet shop. Normally prices are comparable.

Veterinary nurses are always willing to cuddle new puppies, so make the most of the visit by allowing them to make your pup's acquaintance. The vet nurse will know about the availability of puppy groups and training classes in your area. Do remember that this is not the time to introduce your pup to other dogs. Dogs at the surgery are often there because they are ill, perhaps stressed, and so are not in the best frame of mind for meeting puppies.

visitors

Every household has two different types of visitors: those who come because they are friends or family, and those who deliver items or give services to the house such as postmen/women, window cleaners and refuse collectors. The pup needs to understand that these people are allowed to call and should not be feared, barked at or attacked! When the pup is very young, it will be relatively easy to supervise but as it starts to become more sure of itself, it may become a little out of hand unless you set the rules at an early stage.

The best method is to introduce the pup to the various visitors on a lead and in a controlled situation, particularly if it is the boisterous type. The last thing you want is a happy-go-lucky pup bounding all over the visitor and being shouted at or, even worse, hit because the unsuspecting person was not ready for its affections. Faced with even a small pup hurtling towards them, many people (particularly those who have had bad experiences with dogs) will panic, wave their arms around and scream. All these things will excite the dog even more, and it will jump up to try and grab at those things waving around! The more sensitive dog learns that people are to be feared and later this can lead to aggression caused by fear. People also tend to expect the dog to be vicious, especially if you allow uncontrolled greetings and sharp puppy teeth come into contact with soft human skin. Already *you* have created a pup with a reputation for nipping. The next time the pup sees the visitor, the whole situation will be ten times worse; the pup will be more excited and the person will respond even sooner in a desperate attempt to avoid the confrontation.

The solution is to think ahead and set up situations so that you have full control. Do not allow the dog free access to the entrance of your garden or yard where visitors might enter unannounced. Put the dog on its lead, introduce it to the visitor and tell it to 'Sit' while the visitor gives it a titbit.

One of the best things to do is to have a small party. Have some titbits ready, and instruct your guests to collect a morsel for the puppy on their way in. Often you will have to tell your guests how to behave around your puppy. Many people feel the need to bury their heads in the dog's fur, or bend over it. If the puppy is a little unsure this will make it worse. Tell people to stand or sit up straight and not to bend over the animal. People often stare straight into the animal's eyes. This is very unnerving for the pup which may have difficulty dealing with it. Watch for the people who do this, and explain that it is seen by the dog as an act of confrontational dominance, and not something that should be done to any animal.

It is amazing how many visitors seem happy to allow a pup to lick their faces. Normally, telling the visitor of obvious disease risk does not work, but reminding them what else the dog washes with its tongue is enough to make them withdraw in disgust!

Do not allow your puppy to pester anyone unduly. It is acceptable that it says 'Hello' in a controlled manner, but then tell it to lie down or come back to your side where you can control its behaviour.

Child visitors are often a problem because they want to play with the puppy, and at this stage you may not have been able to teach the puppy to play gently without using its teeth. The only way to avoid problems is to be controlled with both child and puppy. Allow a small

Keep your pup on the lead until it understands that visitors are welcome.

amount of *supervised* play, showing the child how to treat the pup. Make sure that the child does not roll around on the floor with the pup, as this will give the pup the idea that it is equal, if not higher, in ranking than the child. The best thing to do is to be constructive and show the child how to train the puppy with titbits, just as you have been doing. Very soon the child will be able to get the pup to go into the sit, down and stand and maybe even follow at heel. This is a good, valuable and constructive experience for both child and pup.

If you have a quieter, more sensitive pup it is best to leave it to come out when it is ready. Encourage it out subtly, by preparing food and putting some nearby, or by rolling a toy on the floor. Avoid direct confrontation and eye-to-eye contact because, as explained above, the dog will

If you do not provide stimulation, the pup will find its own!

take this as a sign that you are exerting dominance over it, or confronting it in a dominant way. The sensitive, more submissive pup is probably quite happy to accept your control without you adding any more power to it!

getting to know your puppy

The better you are at understanding everything about your puppy, the better relationship you will ultimately have, and the better control you will be able to display. Getting to know it is not just about learning when it is going to misbehave, but about knowing every little mood and action. In my experience, the best way to do this is to spend as much time as possible with it, and make sure that much of that time is what might be termed 'quality time'.

These sessions should be instigated by you, so that the pup does not get the idea that it can demand attention at any time. Sit on the floor with it in front of you, and slowly and gently stroke it, touch it and massage its body. Stroke its mouth and head, its legs right down to the feet, between the pads, its inner thighs and its tail from base to tip. Make sure that every part of the pup's body can be touched, and teach it that your attentions are kind and enjoyable. Move your hands in gentle, circular, soothing movements. Your dog may find this a little odd to start with, but persevere as it will help it to relax and make it more aware of its own body.

chapter *twelve*

When your pup is teething, massage its gums, just as you might a baby. These sessions will not only help the pup to relax, but they will also help *you* to relax with your dog.

the first few months

In its first few months with you, the puppy is starting to feel its feet and enjoying new experiences. The more experiences it has, the better it will become at coping with, and adapting to, new situations.

It is important that the relationship of the dog with the family develops in the correct and most appropriate way, and for many months to come you should continue to go through training routines and control exercises as outlined above and in chapter 17 if you wish to maintain the control of your growing pup.

attention seeking

Now the pup is discovering that you are to be trusted, it may become a little over-attentive and pester you or other family members. This can happen to anyone who gives the pup attention and often happens, perhaps surprisingly, with people who are *not* at home with the pup all the time. If someone has been out at work, college or school, naturally the pup rushes to see them when they come home and the most likely response it will get is one of affection. You must be careful that this does not progress into the pup demanding and getting attention regularly, as the next step from this is a dominance struggle.

Therefore, it is important that the pup learns that humans do not respond every time it approaches, and that it must do something for the human before the human responds to its request. This is a good rule for all the family to live by. Observe the family and make sure that they are all following this rule, especially children. Also everyone should make the dog regularly (at least every other time) go and lie down instead of pestering them, and then make sure it has settled or become distracted before they respond to its needs.

If you have a more submissive puppy, you can afford it more privileges but, even so, as the pup approaches adolescence you should withdraw and restrict some of these privileges, just to make sure it knows where it stands in the social structure of the household.

always in trouble!

Sometimes, as puppies become more sure of themselves, they get more adventurous. If you are having difficulties preventing inappropriate behaviour, it is useful to attach a house lead to your puppy's collar (assuming it has learned about a lead and collar already). This lead can be made at home from cheap, light-weight rope or line, approximately 1.8–3m (6–10ft) long. This makes it easier to control the pup, because the lead trails behind and you can catch it more easily. Thus you can make sure that the pup behaves correctly, for instance, when visitors arrive, or if it has developed a bad habit. If it chews the line simply knot it and do not worry. However, you should not leave the line on the pup if you are not there in case it gets tangled. This is also very useful if the dog decides that it is more fun to run away than to come back to you when out for a walk. Gradually you can dispense with the line, but it serves as a remote extension to your arm, and helps to give you the confidence to train the pup with a pleasant attitude.

social training

'mad half hour'

Many puppies, or rather their owners, suffer from 'mad half hours'. In practice the session often only lasts a few minutes, but sometimes it feels like half an hour! The pup puts back its ears and races at top speed around tables, chairs, people, the cat, around the kitchen, into the garden, and then, just for good luck, does another lap or two! There are various reasons for this behaviour – it may be pent-up energy as it often occurs in the evening, a time when the pup would be naturally more active if it were in the wild. Generally, it is just a thing that puppies do.

Nine-week-old Sally investigates life in the garden. Photograph by Mrs K Dorfgar

When my pups do it I allocate it a keyword and put it under my control. If you do this, eventually you can instigate the behaviour by attitude and command. If you do not want the behaviour then ignore it, as pups normally grow out of it. Certainly it is not a good idea to scold the pup because this just draws attention to the act, and builds up more frustrations.

'spooky' puppies

As the pup starts to grow up, even with the best social training there may be things that make it nervous. An unusual noise, a strange shape in a familiar setting, a sudden movement, or a person, animal or vehicle coming apparently from nowhere are all things that might startle the puppy, and then what sort of reaction you get depends on its character. It may try to run away, or stand its ground, bark, growl, or it may chase and snap. Often this behaviour comes as a complete surprise to the owner, who blames all sorts of things in his ignorance.

chapter *twelve*

'Staffy', the Staffordshire Bull Terrier, relaxes after a romp.   Photograph by Robert Smith

Sometimes the behaviour seems unpredictable, and sometimes it is – to us. Often changes or developments in behaviour coincide with adolescence. The pup is now growing up and nature has provided it with the power to learn and to become increasingly sensitive to environment and change. We are far less sensitive than the dog and do not always realise what might startle the pup. Take the case of the unfortunate jogger. Ignored by the pup previously, today he is wearing bright red clothes, red – a warning colour in the animal kingdom. Or that same jogger suddenly decides to look the pup right in the eye – a dominant stare. The pup may have only seen the moving feet before but today it sees the eyes – it must react. It is an animal; it will react in the instinctive or learned way that comes first to its mind, without stopping to think what might be most appropriate or what the humans might prefer.

To counteract these particular problems, we must teach the dog to trust us and to look to us when unfamiliar situations present themselves. Recognising the fact that the pup is 'spooking' is the most important factor, and the next step is then dealing with it in a controlled manner.

In some situations it will be appropriate to go up to the object that the pup is frightened of to show it that there is nothing to worry about. Take your time and encourage the pup with food. Try not to make a big deal out of the whole thing. If it has spooked at something in particular, go and stand by the object, pat it, talk to it; ignore the pup which soon will come over to see that there is nothing to be feared. If it does not come to investigate, do not force it, simply walk away and try again tomorrow.

It is not always possible to approach the object which is the cause of the anxiety and so you need to teach the dog to turn away from frightening things and look to you for comfort and an alternative reaction.You have been teaching the pup to play on your keyword 'Play', and this is a situation where you will be able to use this word. Find a special toy that the dog really likes, and teach it to turn to this on command. A good way to train this is to walk along with the dog on lead, then suddenly turn in the opposite direction and produce the toy. Enthusiastically encourage your dog in the opposite direction. Have some tasty treats with you too and give it one of these. When you have perfected this procedure in a safe area such as the garden, go to a place where the dog might want to look at something, but not where it would be unduly frightened, and test your training. Have it on lead and, as it looks away, say 'Play', reel in its lead, giving playful little jerks on the lead to encourage it, turn around and start walking briskly in the opposite direction. If your training has been good, the pup will want to turn to you and the toy.

Continue this training regularly, and do not wait for a difficult situation to occur. When out with the dog, always be fully aware of what is going on around you and, when a situation does arise that is potentially frightening, be ready to react *before* the dog does. If you keep alert, soon the pup will learn that, when it sees things it does not understand, it can turn to you for reassurance and guidance, and your walks together will be much more fun.

personal protection

Do not worry that in following the above procedure you will eliminate any guarding behaviour the dog might have. Quite the contrary will happen, in fact. You are teaching the dog to be confident. If you need the dog to protect you because of a potentially difficult situation, simply change your attitude to one of alert apprehension, and you will observe the dog's attitude also change immediately.

Do not let your pup barge through doorways!
Photograph by Rod Ware

13 leaving your pup *alone*

Teaching your pup to be on its own is a very important lesson. If done correctly, it will serve you well for the rest of your dog's life but, if approached in an incorrect manner, it can have a serious effect on both of you.

Two of the major problem areas that cause dog owners to call on behavioural consultants or dog trainers are chewing or destructive behaviour, and howling or barking when the owner is out. The latter is one of the common reasons for dogs being sent to rescue centres; the owners just cannot cope with the problems any more, and may have suffered complaints from neighbours or, worse, had official notices served on them because of the noise their dog made when it was left alone.

All this can be avoided if care is taken in the pup's initial training, and even older dogs can be re-conditioned to behave more acceptably if the owners follow a training programme to teach them to accept and be confident.

It is a great trauma for the dog when it comes home with you and leaves the security and warmth of the only thing it has ever known. It will attach itself mentally and physically to anything or anyone who shows it safety and comfort, and feeds it. If suddenly all goes quiet, and the only companions it has managed to find now disappear, it will call out in dog language to say, 'I'm here, where are you?' In many cases it will continue to call until you come

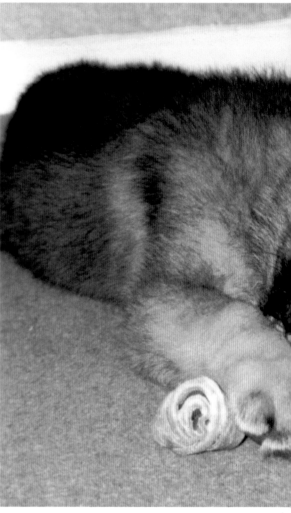

Give the pup something to keep it occupied. Bodie was photographed by Leigh Furey

back. Even if you are not very pleasant when you arrive, you are all it has got, so if you then disappear once more it will continue to call until you return or until it exhausts itself.

It is better to be prepared to take the dog around with you and gradually teach it that it is all right to be alone than to abandon it and listen to its distressed crying. It could be argued that a new-born human baby can be left in a room alone, but this tends to be after he has been rocked to sleep, or is preoccupied. When he awakes and finds no one there, he cries until the parents return and comfort him. It takes a while to teach the baby to be alone with his own thoughts and fears whilst he is awake, and a good mother finds things to take the baby's mind off the fact that he is by himself.

Puppies are the same. They whimper, howl and bark to communicate to their pack which, in the absence of other dogs, is you! Later, if you do not condition the dog, its anxiety will show itself in other ways and it may well become destructive. It may start to urinate or defecate whereas it was clean before or, if it is a very young pup, it may be very difficult to get clean because of the effect of anxiety on its bodily functions. Its mental development will be affected and you are creating a problem dog. Remember that the dog is a pack animal and it is a great wrench for it to be alone and, in fact, very cruel to leave it for long periods.

Select an area where, later on when you are going out without the dog, it will be unable to see you go as seeing you leave will heighten its anxiety level. Also try to choose an area where the dog can be left to its own devices and cannot do much damage to your property or to itself and which can be easily cleaned and no one will be annoyed if its bladder (or worse) lets it down,.

Dogs like a cosy corner or an area that feels secure. Crates are a great idea, because they have the added benefits of helping the dog to be clean – it will not want to foul its own bed area. If restricted to the crate, the pup will be more inclined to hold itself until released, as long as this is not an unreasonably long time. A crate will stop the dog running around and getting excited, and also prevent it from having access to the wrong things which it could start chewing. Training the pup to go in its crate is covered in chapter 8.

Once you have selected your area, place the dog's bed, blanket or crate there. Choose a key word that in the future will mean 'go to this area', for instance 'Bed', 'Crate' or 'Blanket'. Encourage the dog into the area, tell it the key word, and use a chew or treat to get it to go down. Stay with the pup and wait for it to finish the treat. Call it away from the area, and then start the whole procedure again.

Next choose a time when the dog is tired, take it to the area, and encourage it to lie down with a chew. Sit on a chair near it and read a book. Ignore the pup if it pesters you, and eventually it will lie down and go to sleep. Leave it to sleep for a while, and then wake it. Reward the pup with another treat and then go about your business, staying in its vicinity but ignoring it. Take no notice if it comes up to you (this is the hard bit), and eventually it will either settle back down or find something else to do.

The reason why you are ignoring it is to lessen its dependency on you. Obviously you would intervene if it got into difficulties, but it must learn that you are not always at its beck and call. Once you have spent some time on your own business then you can play with it. Find a toy and start a game, but do not forget you must also finish the game yourself, and not allow the dog to gain possession of the toy (see chapters 11 and 16).

When the dog is going about its business again and you are doing the same, watch for it getting tired. Choose this time to take it back to the bed area with a chew or treat and repeat the first stage, getting it into a 'down' on its bed. As soon as it is preoccupied with a chew, go out of the room and then come straight back. Reward the pup with a special treat and then ignore it again. If it is sufficiently interested in its chew, go out of the room again, this time closing the door, but immediately return and praise the dog or give it another treat. This is enough for one session.

Continue training later the same day or the next day. Go back to stage one, because if you start where you left off the dog will, in most cases, become confused and your training will go backwards instead of forwards. Once the pup is happily on its bed chewing and you have stayed in the same room with it, give it another treat or chew toy, and go out of the room for a moment, come back, reward, go out, close the door, come back, reward. Continue to do this for a few moments and then stay with the dog for a while, ignoring it. Go back and reward and then go out, again closing the door, but this time staying out a few moments longer than before. Come back and reward.

If the dog starts to become distressed, you are progressing too fast or staying away too long. The dog should be becoming blasé about your coming and going. Do several training sessions a day, and increase the time that the dog is left alone in the room. By now it should be so used to going on to its bed or into its crate that it will do it by choice, and it will do so by your command. Eventually you will be able to send the pup to its bed from another room. To start with, take it yourself. As it gains confidence follow it to make sure it goes and give it a reward. You are creating a good association with this bed area, and the dog will be confident and pleased to be there.

Little by little, build the time that the dog is alone while you are in the next room. Soon you can leave it for five, ten, fifteen minutes. Even when you have attained a longer time, go in sooner now and again and reward it for good behaviour. Once you get over the anxiety barrier, or if by following this programme carefully you are able to prevent anxiety, the time lapse will be less important.

Do not wait until you *have* to leave the pup to test your training. Set up the situation, go out of the house and then come back in, and reward it, just as you did when you were only in the next room. Once again, slowly and carefully build the time that it is left, and only leave it when it is settled and confident. Aim for success all the time.

It is a good idea to leave on a radio or the television for the dog. This helps to blank out any external noises that might worry it and also helps to disguise the void that you have left behind. If suddenly all goes quiet in a normally noisy household, the pup is bound to be worried and will become anxious. In some cases it is beneficial to leave a tape recording of the household or of the owner talking, but if you carry out the training correctly it is unlikely that you will need to go to this length.

Choose the right sort of chew toy for when the dog is to be left for longer periods. Make sure that the toy is safe and is designed to be a chew. There are a few available commercially that are designed for this purpose. If you can find a hollow chew toy, stuff it with treats and bits of meat, and this will keep the pup occupied for hours, until eventually it falls asleep.

You should save your chew toys for just this purpose. Do not leave them scattered around for the pup to have at any time; save them for when you leave it, and pick them up when you return. This way they are always fresh to the dog, who is far less likely to become

Your pup must learn to be left alone.
Photograph by Kathy Dorfgar

bored with them and look for other things to chew, or become distressed.

As the dog matures you will be able to incorporate other key words that it understands such as 'Settle' or 'Bed', which will tell it to go and lie down and not to pester. You will even be able to say these words from the other side of the door as you leave, so reminding the dog that it should withdraw and not seek your attention at that point. This will not be a threat, but something that the dog has come to understand and accept as part of life.

Whenever the dog is left alone you should always make adequate allowances for its needs. To expect an adult dog to last more than four hours alone in a house is not fair. To expect a puppy to last this long is even less fair. A couple of hours is plenty for a pup, once it has gone through its training and is happy to be left. If you know that you will have to leave the dog longer on regularly, then you should consider getting it both a companion and an outside enclosure, so that it can at least attend to its bodily functions and let off steam as and when necessary.

grooming your *pup*

Grooming your puppy has three important functions: firstly it keeps the coat clean and free from debris, secondly it acts as a social exercise, teaching the pup that it is all right for its owner to touch it all over, and thirdly it serves as an early warning system, alerting you to anything out of the ordinary in relation to your dog's body.

You should be on the look out for common problems such as skin pests (fleas, ticks), skin allergies, and interdigital cysts (swellings between the toes which can be painful, and may alarm you when they burst if you are not aware of them). You will also notice less common problems that might develop into more serious threats, such as unusual lumps and growths. If you are accustomed to the feel of your dog's body, anything out of the ordinary will be obvious to you, and you will be able to seek veterinary advice if necessary and possibly prevent more serious problems.

Therefore, even if you have a smooth-coated dog such as a Dobermann or Bull Terrier, you should still groom regularly, that is, a minimum of twice a week if not more. With a medium-coated dog, grooming is necessary two to three times a week, and a longer or heavier-coated dog such as the Bearded Collie, Old English, Afghan or Bichon Frise, needs to be groomed at least once a day if you want to avoid expensive grooming salon bills and keep your pet feeling comfortable.

Sometimes grooming salons are asked to shave off the coats of dogs such as the Golden Retriever in the summer because they get too hot. This is not a good idea because the coat actually protects the dog from the heat. To avoid problems, groom thoroughly to remove all the dead hair which, if left, forms a barrier which prevents the air from circulating, thus causing skin irritations and overheating. It is most important that you pay particular attention to areas that tend to mat easily: behind the ears, inside the elbows, tail, chest, stomach and inside the back legs. To make sure that your pet is groomed correctly and not just surface groomed, part the hair back to the skin when brushing.

grooming equipment

You need various tools to groom your pet's coat properly. While it is very young, a soft brush and fine comb is best as its skin is delicate. Later you may need a slicker brush, rake, dematting comb, body glove or other more specialised tools depending on the coat type. It is best to take advice from a qualified groomer or your breeder.

Smooth/skin-coated dogs: As a general guideline, smooth-coated dogs such as the Boxer, Dobermann or Bull Terrier and even the heavier-coated dogs such as the Rottweiler are best groomed with a rubber hound glove to remove dead hair and then finished off with a horse hair hound glove to give the coat a shine. A good tip with smooth dogs like these is to rub over their coats with a chamois leather as this brings any skin cells and scurf to the surface.

grooming your pup

Short double-coated dogs: Dogs such as the Labrador that have a thick undercoat and a waterproof outer coat are best brushed with a slicker brush, followed by a medium-toothed comb, and then finished off with a rubber hound glove.

Longer and/or double-coated dogs: These include Golden Retrievers, German Shepherds and Border Collies. A pin brush is needed if you want to show the dog or a slicker brush if you want it as a pet. The slicker is most efficient, but unfortunately removes a lot of coat and this, of course, is not desirable in the show dog. A rake or dematting rake removes dead hair.

Grooming is a most important part of health care.

Spaniel types: While the puppy is young, use a fine-toothed comb and slicker brush on the feathering as it develops. Also use both of these on the ears. Finger pluck the puppy's fluff hair when it starts to lift at about eight or nine months. Do not allow your groomer to clip as this ruins the coat.

Wire-haired breeds: Dogs such as Fox Terriers, Border Terriers and Schnauzers all require stripping in the spring and autumn when the coat is naturally falling out. This can be left to the professional salon or you can do it yourself. You pluck the dead hair out of the coat using your finger and thumb or a stripping knife.

Dogs with feathering: Many breeds have feathering on their legs and/or tails which, irrespective of the needs of other areas of the body, require specific grooming. The best equipment for feathering is a slicker brush to get rid of the knots and debris followed by a wide toothed comb to remove any further dead hair and finish off.

Woolly coats: Breeds such as the Poodle, Bichon, Bedlington and so on are very popular because they do not shed, but this does not mean that they should not be groomed. On the contrary, they need daily grooming with a slicker brush to prevent matting.

Folded skin: Pay particular attention to folds in the skin by gently wiping them clean, especially after the dog has been eating. A Boxer is an example of a dog with folded skin, and the Shar-Pei, of course, needs extra care!

grooming salons

If you have chosen a breed of dog that requires professional grooming, then you should find a good grooming salon as soon as possible in order to introduce your puppy and to get it used to what it will have to undergo. Also, good salon proprietors will tell you how best to care for your pup's coat in order to make their job easier. This will have an effect on your pocket and the dog's stress level, because a well-cared-for coat will not need as much attention in the salon as a neglected one. It is worth taking the time to get some professional advice in order to save trouble later.

It is best to inspect a number of salons for yourself. Standards of hygiene should be good, staff should be happy and obviously caring, and animals being attended to should not be unduly stressed or anxious. Obviously the dog's state of mind will be affected by its upbringing and the care given by the owner in preparing it for the experience. Some may well look a little 'hang dog' or anxious, especially if they have to experience a long and traumatic session due to their owner's neglect or lack of forethought. But you should see others who are not concerned and, in general, are enjoying all the fuss and pampering. With training and careful preparation, your pup should be one of the ones that enjoys the experience.

Salon staff should be qualified, or at least under the supervision of a qualified person. In the United Kingdom the only recognised qualification is City and Guilds, and this certificate should be displayed on the wall of the salon.

Beware of the salon where the staff ask few questions and are more interested in assuring you of their cheap rates. The salon staff need to assess many things about your pup before quoting a price, and you should ensure what this price includes. Good salons will pay attention to ears and nails as part of the service, and give you advice on coat care and so on. Bad salons could ruin a potentially beautiful coat, for instance, by clipping when the coat should be hand stripped.

If you are not sure whether the advice given by the salon is correct, ask your breeder what procedures are necessary for your particular breed, and then make sure that the salon is aware and prepared to follow these guidelines.

care of feet

Feet are often neglected in the grooming process, but as they are the parts that come into most contact with the outside world, they are probably the most likely places for problems to occur. With smooth-coated dogs it is easy to see any debris, stones or seeds caught between the toes or in the pads. It is not so easy with heavy or longer-coated dogs, and careful examination is required to make sure that no foreign bodies are trapped in the hair or between the pads. Too much hair left between the toes and pads of hairy dogs such as the Cocker Spaniel may well cause the foot to splay out. It is a good idea to trim hairy feet, unless you intend to show and your breed standard requires that you do not do so. It enhances the general appearance of the dog, and also helps to make it much easier for you to detect any problems which might occur.

For the best results, you need a pair of trimming scissors (round-ended, curved trimming scissors give you extra safety if you are a little nervous), and a pair of thinning scissors. Use the ordinary trimming scissors to trim the hair between the pads. Open up the toes to give you access to the hair between them, and trim carefully, close to the skin. The hair on the top of the foot is best trimmed with the thinning scissors. Pull it up away from the foot, hold the scissors parallel with the foot, and then scissor through. If you have a breed with webbed feet take great care that you do not catch the webbing.

You can also remove the hair on the hocks with the thinning scissors if you want to. With breeds such as the Bearded Collie and Old English you can still have the rounded appearance by lifting the top hair and checking for mats and knots between the toes, and then combing the top hair down, and trimming the foot round at ground level.

preparing the grooming area

To begin with it is best if there is someone with you to steady the pup, especially if it is a large breed, and the whole process should be taken slowly, firmly and kindly. A supply of titbits is always a good idea to help retain the confidence of the pup.

If you can, arrange to have the pup on a sturdy table with a non-slip surface (carpet or rubber matting is ideal). This makes the task much easier, and is a physical signal to the dog that it must not get over-excited. It is not ideal to groom and clip nails on the floor as the dog is used to playing with you there, and it may take a while to get it to understand that it must stay still. The elevated, false position on the table helps the pup to differentiate straight away.

Choose a time when the pup is not full of energy, as this is an exercise of confinement, and it is better for both of you if the dog is naturally relaxed and subdued before starting.

chapter *fourteen*

A non-slip surface makes the pup feel safe.

training the pup for general grooming

Care must be taken to make the experience as pleasurable and non-traumatic as possible.

Step one: Put the pup on the table and give it a reward. Hold it close to your body so that it gains security from you, as this first stage may be a little frightening for it. Have your equipment on the table and a supply of treats at the ready. Take your time.

Step two: Show the pup your soft brush if it is not too big in relation to it, or show it a comb. Allow it to sniff at the tool and give it a reward so that it has a good association.

Step three: Hold the pup close and gently glide the comb through its coat. Give a reward.

Step four: Repeat step three but groom a different place.

Step five: Build up the time and places that you can groom, without causing stress. If the dog becomes tired or agitated, calm it and leave the job to another session.

If you are working alone, offer the pup a hide chew that will keep it occupied longer than individual titbits and, as long as you have built up trust, it will be happy to let you continue.

nail clipping

Nail clipping can be a delicate business and many dog owners shy away from doing this themselves. However, you should have no problem at all if you start when your pup is young. Left for some time, the nails grow long, and the young dog unaccustomed to having its nails clipped may become very distressed and struggle, making the task difficult and upsetting for all concerned.

There is a large range of nail clippers on the market to suit all tastes. In my experience the best and easiest to use are the type designed to allow the nail to be supported all around.

These tend not to squeeze the nail and are simple to use. It might be worth having a compound to hand which will stop bleeding should you be unfortunate and cut the quick, and this is available from vets and good pet shops or grooming salons. It is sometimes necessary to file rough edges of nails especially on very young puppies, or to give the finishing touches to the show dog's feet, and for this you can use an ordinary 'human' nail file.

Inside the nail is the vein, often referred to as the 'quick'. This shows up very easily if your pup's nails are white or clear. It cannot be seen with black nails and so you must take extra care, cutting a tiny bit at a time. Often pups have some of each colour and the white ones help as a guideline. However, remember the vein may not be in the same position in every nail, because the nails grow at irregular rates or some may be worn down more than others. If the nail is left, the quick grows longer; if this has been allowed to happen, you will have to trim a little each day until the quick recedes to a more normal level.

Train your dog from an early age to sit quietly on the table to be groomed.

training the pup for care of the feet

Step one: Put the pup on the table and give it a reward, holding it close to your body so that it gains security from you. This stage may be a little less frightening if you have already done some training for general grooming but you must still take your time to avoid creating problems.

Step two: Hold each paw in turn with a firm grip, without pinching, and offer a reward. Look at the toes and see where the quick is and decide where you will make your first cuts. Have your clippers on the table and allow the pup to sniff at them, assuring itself that they are not a threat.

Step three: Go through the procedure again, this time with the clippers in your hand.

chapter fourteen

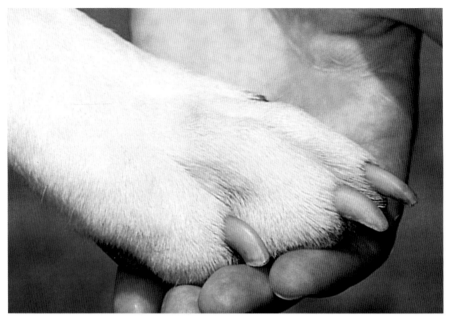

Clip the nail just at its tip so that you do not cut the quick. Photograph by Robert Smith

Step four: Pick up a paw, look for the quick and, if it is visible, place the cutter over the nail, clip it away and then reward the dog. If there is no quick visible, place the clippers onto the tip of the nail, and take just a small piece off the end.

Step five: Pick up another paw, look for the quick, place the cutter over the nail, clip just short of the quick, and reward.

Step six: Your helper, if you have one, could use the titbits to distract the dog's attention while you pick up a paw and clip a few nails. If you are on your own, clip as many as you can on one paw, making sure that the pup does not get distressed. A hide type chew might serve the purpose as the pup will take time to chew on this and by now it will be less bothered about what is going on around its feet.

Step seven: Take your time to build up to clipping all four paws. If your pup starts to get bored or distressed, finish off and complete the task later. You can be quite controlled with the dog, and give it back the chew if it drops it to look at what you are doing, but do not enter into a battle with it. It is better to stop attending to the nails and make the pup do a 'down' with a treat, taking away the intensity of the situation. Come back to the task later on when the pup has had a run around, and got rid of some energy.

Remember that it is best to cut your pup's nails regularly, to keep them in trim and so that your pup is not frightened if suddenly you decide they need doing.

grooming your *pup*

NB: Don't forget that most dogs have dew claws on the side of each front foot, and some have them on the hind legs as well. These need to be trimmed in the same way as all the other nails, and may well be longer because they do not get the same wear. As the dog matures and is active it may be the case that nails wear down naturally, but you will always have to pay attention to these dew claws.

ear care

As part of your regular grooming sessions, you should always check your pup's ears. To clean dirty ears, pour a few drops of almond oil on to a small swab of cotton wool and gently wipe away the dirt and debris. Any reddy/brown waxy substances or smelly discharges should be taken seriously as they may indicate infection or infestation of ear mites, and you should get veterinary advice as soon as possible. It is best not to try to diagnose and treat problems yourself, as you may make matters worse.

oral hygiene

A healthy pup has a healthy mouth, and therefore you should check inside for abnormalities as the teeth develop, and for any tooth decay or gum infection. Sometimes the puppy teeth remain in the gums even after the adult teeth come through. Chewing and tugging games may dislodge the unwanted teeth, but veterinary help may be necessary to rectify the problem as the retention of milk teeth can affect the growth of the permanent teeth.

Teeth are often neglected, and vets report that many visits to the surgery could be avoided, or at least be less expensive, if more care was taken earlier. Regular brushing with special canine toothpaste or gel and brush will help look after your pup's teeth and gums. This should be started once the pup has its second set of teeth at around nine months of age. Before this, you should open your pup's mouth regularly to get

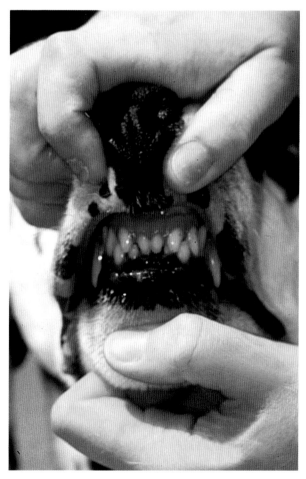

Your pup should get used to having its mouth examined.
Photograph by Robert Smith

it used to having its mouth looked at and touched. You can get a tool called a 'tooth scaler' to clean away tartar from your pet's teeth, but you can do more harm than good if you are not sure what you are doing, so it is best to seek professional guidance.

The Nylabone range of dog chews are specially formulated to help prevent tartar and promote good dental hygiene.

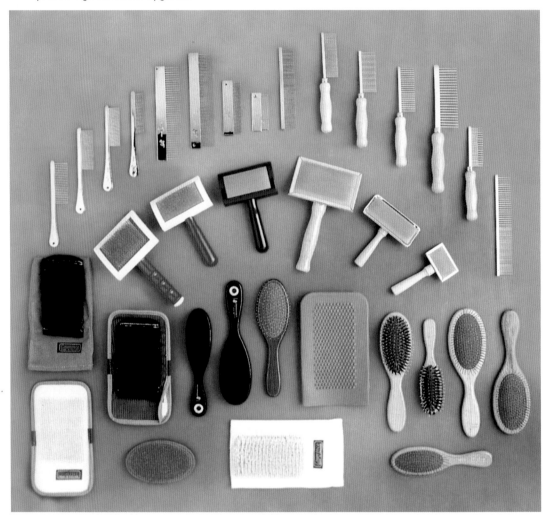

A complete range of brushes, combs, scissors and clippers. You will need only one or two of these to look after your dog – ask your breeder or local salon staff which are most suitable.
Photograph reproduced by courtesy of Allbrooks Products Ltd (Animal Grooming Products).

eyes
For many dogs a small clear discharge from the eye seems normal because of the shape of the eye and eyelid. Some breeds, such as the Bichon Frise, Poodle or Lhasa Apso, suffer from problems of discharge from the eyes. This is a particular problem for light-coloured dogs as it

looks unsightly. Preparations are available from the pet shop or grooming salon that help to reduce staining on the fur, but these need to be used regularly from the start to be effective. If you do not attend to the discharge each day it can become encrusted around the dog's eye, leading to discomfort, distress and sore patches when you try to get it off. The eyes should be bathed daily with a dilute solution of saline soaked into cotton wool (one teaspoon of salt to one pint of warm water).

If the discharge is not clear and/or is smelly or like pus, then you should take the dog to the veterinary surgeon for a check up, as the dog may have conjunctivitis or some other eye infection.

anal glands

Some breeds of dog and lines within a breed are prone to problems with the anal glands. These are scent glands which

Regular grooming enables you to check for abnormalities.

are situated under the skin at each side of the anus. They produce a foul-smelling liquid which is normally discharged through a tiny opening at each side of the rectum when hard or bulky food is passed in the form of faeces. This process is less effective when a dog is fed soft foods, and sometimes it requires a little help. This involves gentle pressure to empty the glands but it can cause bruising if it is not done correctly. Therefore it is best to have your vet or an experienced groomer show you how to do this should it be necessary.

There are outward signs of the dog's discomfort that will alert you to its condition. It may scrape its rear end along the ground or suddenly turn around and bite the base of its tail, or constantly lick its anus. If your dog is displaying any of these signs, you should take it to your vet for further advice.

Don't forget: When attending to your dog's hygiene don't neglect your own. *Always* wash your hands before and after examining, grooming, or cleaning any area of your dog's body.

15 children
and dogs

Emily with 12-week-old Zoe.   Photograph by G Lewis

Children and dogs together bring their own set of potential problems. It is often difficult to make some children realise that the puppy is an animal and not an extension or addition to their toy box. From the outset, the rule should be that the puppy is *never* left with a baby or young child in the absence of a suitably experienced and capable adult, not even for a moment! Remember, the puppy is an animal, with animal reactions, and you can never assume that it will always behave in exactly the same way as it has done in the past.

But let us start at the beginning, with babies. In most cases the baby in his cradle or pram is relatively safe from the puppy, simply because the puppy cannot get near the baby. From a social point of view a baby in arms is a very special person. Adults pander to his whims, attend to him when he calls, and feed him on demand. This the pup observes and accepts that the baby is obviously a very high-ranking animal.

children and dogs

The problems more commonly start as the little human becomes more mobile. At this time he is much more vulnerable: he is outside his special bed area, and he has a tendency to get into more trouble with the big humans! In the dog's eyes, therefore, this little human has lost his position of high ranking, if indeed he is even seen to be the same human!

Now the dog has the opportunity it has been waiting for to elevate its own position in the pack. It can help these big humans put the little one in his place! It is not unusual for a dog, without invitation, to try to 'help' the adult human by joining in and attacking the child when the adult scolds him for being naughty. Of course this is not acceptable to us, and the dog needs to learn that the little human, no matter what his failings, is still higher ranking than the dog.

The way to do this is to try to mould the child in the same way that you are moulding the dog, by preventing any incorrect behaviour and guiding the little human into the correct ways so that he can be rewarded and his position maintained. Just as with the dog, the toddler's active mind needs to be occupied and trained, and you will

Children and dogs can be the perfect partnership.
Photograph by Caroline Bell

have your hands full if you are to maintain both a fully occupied child and a fully occupied dog. The answer is to have an area where you can put the dog when you cannot fully concentrate on both. If you feel that you must scold the child, then make sure that the pup is under control first. It is much better to remove the dog to another room.

As the toddler matures you will be able to involve him in the training of the dog, and he

Children's toys are very attractive to puppies.

will learn through watching and participating. Left to their own devices, children will forget what they have been taught, and often make sudden and strange movements and noises. Even if no malice is intended, the dog may react as if it were. Therefore, do not subject your dog to unsupervised young children, because the dog has only its teeth for defence. Always be vigilant, for the sake of your child, your dog, and you!

The older child can participate in the training of the pup straight away. All the techniques are simple and you will find that the control with titbits is the easiest for children. This has the added benefit of telling the dog that the child is in control of the food (see chapters 10 and 17). Do not exclude your children from the training as this will make them feel neglected and less likely to treat the pup with compassion. In addition, it will make the dog feel that it gains attention when the children do not, so leading it to assume another elevation in its position in the hierarchy. If the child is small or unsure, stand behind him to give him confidence. Even toddlers can start training, with your backing, and soon the dog will learn that this little human with the squeaky voice is also in control.

Children's voices tend to be naturally rather high pitched, and on top of this they have a tendency to shriek, run around and wave their arms about. This will excite the pup, so try to teach the child to speak quietly and not to run around the puppy. Of course, children need to let off steam, so this is yet another good reason for having a kennel or crate so that the pup can be contained and accidents prevented. With your guidance, the pup and child will learn how to behave with each other, but do not expect it to happen overnight. Both child and dog will react as their instincts tell them until they have had time to learn other ways.

children and dogs

children's toys

Young children often leave their toys scattered around the floor, and it is very difficult to get over to the pup that these toys do not belong to it. Teaching the dog the keyword 'Leave' will help (see chapter 17), as will teaching the child to tidy up. You need to be ever-vigilant if you do not want the pup to take the toys.

If the pup does pick something up which does not belong to it, call it to you and offer a reward in return for the toy. If it should drop the toy to come to you, that is what you wanted, so reward it. If it goes back to the toy, tell it 'Leave' and follow it to make sure it does so. Don't chase the dog if it is carrying the toy as it will think that this is a good game and do it all the more. Even if you shout, it will still continue – dogs bark when they are having fun, don't they? It may think you are enjoying yourself! It is better to go off and find a reward and call the dog to you. Give it the reward as it gives up the toy.

None of this is easy when you have an active child to contend with as well, but perseverance and a cool head will win in the end.

children and training

If your child is interested in training, The Kennel Club has a section, called the KCJO, especially for 8–18 year olds. A wide range of events are offered to suit every kind of interest and ability, including rallies, quizzes, training sessions and competitions. Each year, there is a Grand Contest at Crufts where titles and trophies are awarded. You can find out more about the KCJO from The Kennel Club (see Useful Addresses).

Do let your child help you with all aspects of the pup's training.

16

how to be
top dog

Even the Border Collie will become dominant if you let it.

Parts of this chapter have been presented elsewhere in the book, but if you have a dominant, or potentially dominant, pup it is essential that you control its lifestyle. Therefore, I have brought together all the relevant points to help you to deal with, overcome or simply prevent dominance.

All too often dog owners only realise, or are told by a professional, that they have a dominant dog when the dog's attitude has started to get out of hand. A grumble over food, or maybe a growl over being moved – worse still, the dog bites, or attempts to, in a similar situation. The warning signs are there long before, if only they had been identified by the dog's owner before it was too late! Often, dog owners allow, or live with, certain behaviours in the excuse of having 'a quiet life', but it soon becomes obvious that life is to be by no means quiet!

Starting out correctly with your puppy should mean that you never experience the trauma of living with an out-of-control dominant dog but, if your pup is destined to be dominant then, believe me, it will have a good try at climbing the hierarchy ladder.

Some breeds of dog have more dominant types amongst their ranks than others. Normally dominance is more prevalent in males and in the breeds that have been created over many generations to be in control of certain situations. For example, breeds which have been selectively bred for fighting, terriers bred for vermin control, or animals whose guarding instincts have been sought after – all these are more prone to dominance than dogs that have been bred specifically as lap dogs. You must be aware, however, that just because you have chosen a breed not known for its dominant traits, this does not mean you will not experience dominance.

Obviously some dogs will be more difficult than others. Some of the more difficult and undesirable tendencies may not be so prominent where a certain line has been selectively bred for domestic or show purposes, but this is not guaranteed. In fact, in some cases the dog's beauty has been at the forefront of the breeder's mind, and tendencies for behavioural traits ignored, or not considered a problem.

Dominance can be a problem for dog owners of any breed if the warning signs go unobserved and/or unheeded, and precautions are not taken. Some people have the uncanny knack of making the most submissive types into dominant dogs.

recognising dominance

Imagine this scene: a quite harmless pup is lying across a doorway in a typical puppy snooze. You and the family are walking carefully around so as not to disturb it. A sleepy eye opens and the pup is reluctant to move, so you decide to leave it 'because he's tired'. The pup has just won its first step on the road to dominance.

A few more similar occurrences and the pup starts to assume control of its new-found power. Soon it falls upon other situations that you allow which shows it that it is the boss.

- It eats its meal in a corner. You think, 'Out of my way.' *'Protected and exclusive,'* thinks the pup.
- The pup gets its food before the rest of the family. You think, 'To keep him quiet.' *'Because I'm boss,'* thinks the pup.
- It finds its toys and starts up games. You think, 'Cute, isn't he.' *'Hey look, they play when I say play now,'* thinks the pup.
- It has its own bed in a corner. You decide, 'Somewhere for him to go out of the way.' *'My own exclusive pad,'* says the pup.
- It climbs onto the furniture, and settles between two people, pushing its way in. 'He pushes in for cuddles.' You think this is cute as well. *'I push humans around,'* – the pup learns that it can push you or other family members out of the way.

I could go on; the number of inadvertent, dominance-building occurrences can be endless. Some people whom I have assisted in the course of my behavioural problem consultancy have an absolute library of 'little happenings' that have mounted up and culminated in the dog being in no doubt at all that *it* was the top dog in the family.

Some of the situations can be much more subtle than those that I have illustrated, and not always easy to spot. For instance, if someone in the household is out a lot, responds to the dog with enthusiasm when he comes home, and follows this up by pandering to the dog all the time, the pup singles this person out for special attention and learns how to control his behaviour. Watch them interacting. If the person looks at the pup, does the pup avert its eyes? It should! Does the pup lick the person excessively? It should not! Does the pup single this person out as a target to get titbits at mealtimes? It probably does – but it shouldn't. If the pup sees everyone as higher ranking than itself, it should not be singling out individuals for activities like these. If the dog singles someone out and simply likes to be around them, then this is quite normal. Usually this is the person who exerts the most control, not aggressively, but by the way that he lives his life. The dog feels comfortable knowing its place with this individual.

A top dog has its exclusive bed area.

Some dogs can be allowed all the scenarios listed above and more, and never be a problem to their owners, often because they have not a dominant nature or because other situations tip the balance and the dog accepts its place. However, given enough of the correct dominance-building situations, most dogs can become dominant to some degree, even if it only shows or is a problem in certain situations.

The dominant stance is often the first sign and learning to recognise it will help you to react quickly. The pup stands square and erect, its ears forward and tail held high. Obviously some breeds naturally stand like this but, if you observe closely, you will see the difference between the passive stance and the dominant one.

understanding dominance

All animals (and domestic dogs are no different) live with two basic motivations, food and sex: in other words, self-preservation and perpetuating the species. Being at the top of the hierarchy is part of the pattern of life that helps to ensure that your genes are the ones that are passed on. If you are in control of situations then you have the first chance to be in the right place at the right time. Survival of the fittest! Of course, in a household situation none of this should apply, but unfortunately we are unable to explain this verbally to the dog.

In its behaviour, whether Chihuahua or German Shepherd, Corgi or Newfoundland, your dog reacts very much like a juvenile wolf, some dogs being born with more built-in programming for potential dominance than others. Your dog reacts to situations as they occur; its mind connects to what happens as it happens. Its memory is different to ours in that it does not think backwards and forwards in the same way that we do, but simply reacts through instinct or learned behaviour to the situation in hand. Therefore there is no point in chastising or, indeed, rewarding behaviour that has happened earlier, even if it was only seconds before, because the dog has no idea to what you are referring unless your actions coincide with its own, exactly as they happen.

We can, however, build up a pattern of behaviour in our dog that informs it that it is no longer in control and that taking the dominant role is not such a good idea. This is done by the way in which we live our lives. We can assert dominance ourselves without *ever* raising our hand or voice to the pup. Handled with aggression, the pup will react to our actions because it feels threatened. We must rise above the very basic urge to control with physical strength and take a much more supreme role in order to ensure that the dog does not start nor, indeed, continue to challenge our authority or that of family and friends.

Aggression from humans is *not* the answer. Indeed, the developing pup will see aggression as a sign that the owner has lost or is losing control, and therefore will attempt to challenge a little harder or a little sooner next time its behaviour is triggered, in the hope that you will be knocked from your shaky pedestal. If it does not feel it can challenge you it may challenge family members or acquaintances whom it considers lower in the pecking order. If it cannot hit out at its oppressor it will, like abused humans, hit out at those who are easier targets.

Follow the guidelines detailed below if you have a dominant or potentially dominant puppy. If it is already showing signs of dominance, you should see a marked difference in the dog's behaviour within 24 hours. The dog will learn by your actions that its place is way down in the hierarchy and the likelihood of a challenge lessens all the time you continue to follow the rules. The more controlled you and your family are, the more successful you will be. If your pup is already showing aggressive dominance to you or any family member then you must be very strict with yourself in the way that you follow the rules.

controlling dominance

Rule one: Do not lie on the floor or furniture and allow the pup to lie on you freely. Take the dominant role by remaining above the pup both physically and mentally. A pup with dominant tendencies will feel very much in control if it is on top of you.

Rule two: Take up all the pup's toys and keep them out of its reach in a drawer or cupboard. These must now remain in *your* possession. Do not feel that you are being mean or depriving the pup, because you will make up for this amply with your attention to training and control. The pup's life will soon become much more fulfilled than it ever was before, because you will have to work hard to keep it under control,.

Rule three: Games must be instigated by you, not the pup. Only play when *you* want to, when *you* feel in control, and when the pup is obviously under the impression that *you* started the game. The pup must not be allowed to think that it started the game – do not pretend to yourself. *You* must win all the games.

Rule four: Do not throw toys and allow the pup to run off and take possession of them. Play should be enjoyed with the dog on the lead under your complete control. If the pup should win by accident, bring it back to you by finding some form of reward that it would like even more than the toy that it has in its possession, such as a different toy or titbit. Always have something in your pocket to aid you in control. Encourage the pup to sit, go down or do some other control exercise for the reward, and then you have regained control.

Rule five: If you are playing tug games, use a titbit in conjunction with the keyword 'Leave' to get the pup to release on command. Avoid tug games until you know you can win.

Being allowed to act like a human can lead to dominance.

Rule six: Do not allow the pup to become obsessive over games that it plays on its own. Discourage any repetitive or stereotypic actions by distracting it onto other things. Stereotypic behaviour is the type of behaviour that can be seen in some zoo animals, that is, repetitive, seemingly meaningless actions often heightened by excitement and frustration. Animals need plenty of stimulating activities and varying environments to prevent this behaviour. Allowing this behaviour to carry on often results in aggression when its drive is interrupted.

Rule seven: Do not allow the pup to stare at you eye to eye. If it has this tendency, make it look away before you do by distracting it with your hand or a toy. Then ignore it, act naturally and do not instigate a stare-out if you can avoid it.

Rule eight: Do not allow the dog to demand attention for any reason, even if it is to attend to its bodily functions such as food or toilet. Anticipate its needs and organise events so that you can make it do something else, or so that it is busy doing something else when *you* tell it that it is time for toilet, food or bed.

Rule nine: Do not position its bed in an area that it can easily guard, such as a cosy corner of a room. If it is displaying guarding or dominance tendencies over its bed, call it out of the room the first few times that you move the bed to avoid confrontation. Move the bed regularly; make sure that the pup allows you to go freely into its bed area and do this several times a day at least.

Rule ten: Do not allow the pup free access to your bed area, to the entrance to your bedroom, or even to the hall or landing leading to your bed. Top dogs have an exclusive bed area, so make sure that yours is exclusive to you, and that the pup's bed area is readily available to all of the family.

Rule eleven: Do not allow the pup to barge through doorways ahead of you. This may mean restricting access for the pup until it is trained. Use your lead to make sure you have control of the pup, make it sit and then you go through the doorway first. Top dogs inspect the surroundings first, so make sure *you* are top dog.

Rule twelve: Top dogs make it obvious to their pack that they have the option of eating first.

Rottweilers have a high incidence of dominance but can still be controlled.

Feed your pup after you and your family have eaten. If this is not possible, make sure the pup sees you eating something while you are preparing its meal, even if you have to pretend to eat the dog food! If the situation is such that the pup has been fed before the family, put it in another room or outside, so that it does not watch you eat while it sits there with a full stomach.

Rule thirteen: Do not allow the pup to eat in a corner of a room. If its food dominance is getting out of hand (it is growling or snarling over food), you may need to change the room in which you feed it, thus giving you fresh ground and the leading stance.

Rule fourteen: Teach the pup that you are in control of food by following this simple training procedure. Prepare the food in a bowl. Offer a morsel of food on a small dish separately, keeping control of the main dish. When the first offering is eaten with no growling or aggression, offer another piece. Continue this process until all the meal is eaten. Bringing the dish back to replenish it teaches the pup that you are more likely to give food than take it away. If there is any sign of growling or aggression, withdraw and offer no more food. Try again later.

You may find better control if you change the room where you feed and put the dog under the control of its lead. The pup will soon learn that you are in control of the food and that you offer more food when it responds correctly. Once you are confident, allow the pup a little more food at a time and alternate this with putting the dish on the floor.

Each member of the family, including children, should learn this procedure. It is important that the pup sees that all the family is above it in the hierarchy, but do not put your children at risk of being bitten. First have complete control of the pup yourself, and supervise your children. Make sure the pup is aware that you are backing the children. Instruct the child, allowing him to watch you first and then stand immediately behind him to guide and give confidence. Do not get cross with the child, as the pup may think it is its duty to help you (the top dog) to chastise the underling (child).

Rule fifteen: Train your pup using the techniques described in chapter 17, and make sure that you are able to maintain full control at all times. Continue to train the pup on a regular basis, even after you believe it understands what is required. Repeating the training procedures will help you to maintain top class control of your dog.

keeping good control

• *Do not* be afraid of putting the pup on a lead, even in the house, when situations are likely to be at their most difficult or when you feel you need added control. This may be especially important at the start of training, when visitors are expected or any other time that you need complete control or extra confidence. Always have something handy to use as a reward for the pup's good behaviour and to encourage good conduct.

• *Do not* threaten the dog into the control exercises; it should be firmly controlled, yet taught in a friendly, non-aggressive manner.

• *Do not* avoid situations that the pup does not like, or where it has shown signs of dominance or aggression, but do not put yourself in a situation where you risk being bitten. Alter the circumstances so that you can take control and feel confident in handling the situation. Work back to problem areas, slowly building up your own confidence.

This pup has a natural instinct to retrieve, but you must make sure that it learns what it is allowed to pick up. Photograph by Mrs J Pryor

- *Do not* be too predictable or over-repetitive in your daily routine or training programme. If you do, an intelligent pup will soon start to try to take the lead role, anticipating your next move.

- *Do* teach your pup to accept and enjoy being groomed (see chapter 14). If it does not like it, distract it with a toy or titbit and start very gently with a soft brush, building up the volume of the area that you cover each day until you can touch the whole of your pup's body. Grooming is a very natural part of a pup's social behaviour and it must learn to accept being groomed by you.

- *Do* make sure that your pup has plenty of activities which involve your control: training sessions, games started by you, changes of environment, excursions to new places, and so on. This will stimulate its mind to accept your control and use up excess energy.

- *Do* stick to the rules if you want to maintain control of your dominant or potentially dominant dog.

The potential to be dominant will not go away; you must control it and remain in control at all times. A strong, fit dog will take any opportunity it can to increase its position in the hierarchy.

essentials of
control

A pup does not come ready programmed to do as it is told by humans. It has no idea what the meanings of the human sounds are, but it is receptive and forever learning. All that remains is that we are patient, understanding and pleasant, and that we teach the pup the meaning of a few simple words in a way that it can understand.

Control is essential for all breeds.

why train your dog?

Most people consider it important to train the dog to obey basic commands, but not everyone finds it easy to be more structured about training. In spite of our intervention in selective breeding programmes, the dog is still primarily a wolf, like its ancestors. Left to its own devices, it will react in wolf-like ways, albeit in a juvenile sense. In many ways, this does not fit into a domestic environment. Because of the adaptability of the wolf, which has become our dog, we have been able to adjust its behaviour, through a process of conditioning, to fit in with our needs.

Many owners seem to think that the pup will learn the rules with very little input from themselves. You will be very lucky if this is the case. In most cases, the education of the puppy needs considerable input from *all* members of the family. Sometimes the family will think back and fondly remember a previous much-loved pet who behaved impeccably. Well, like humans, dogs are all different. Even within a litter, the pups will have different characters. The old dog had over the years learned the idiosyncrasies of the family and how to fit in like the proverbial 'old shoe'. When a new pup comes on the scene, things certainly liven up.

Dogs, like humans, need stimulation. They need to have their active minds and bodies stimulated and trained in the right direction. A bored puppy will be labelled as a mischievous

Toys are great motivators: you can keep control *and* join in the fun. Photo courtesy of John Barron

or downright naughty puppy, and lack of forethought, training and control on your part may lead to disaster. The dog's whole attitude to life and living with the family will depend on the work that you and all of the family put into the training.

Training your dog should be a pleasure, not a chore. Make up your mind *now* to keep control, and to look ahead to all eventualities. Yes, you will make mistakes, but don't blame the dog for *your* errors. Simply count to ten, take a deep breath, and start again.

who should do the training?

Everyone should participate in the training of the dog if it is to be a part of the family structure. It needs to understand that it does not follow rules in the presence of just one member, but that all the family has the control and ability to train and handle it.

In practice, this often means that one person gets to grips with techniques and training exercises first, and then teaches everyone else. Dogs are very adaptable and soon learn if one human is less consistent than another. In the long run, this is making a rod for your own back, as the dog learns to perform correctly for some and not for others. This often causes arguments within the family, resulting in comments like, 'Have you seen what YOUR dog has done while you were out?' Funny how the dog suddenly becomes someone else's property when it does not conform to the ideal!

Often people think that the dog is more likely to 'behave' for the man of the house because he has a more authoritative voice. In fact, dogs take more kindly to gentle voices (remember that the dog's hearing is 16 times more acute than our own), and the majority of top handlers in Obedience Competitions are women. (Perhaps this is because training dogs is very much like training children, and women tend to do most of this.)

chapter *seventeen*

It is important that everyone is aware of the rules, makes sure that the dog follows them, and enters actively into the constructive training programme. Yes, even the children can control the dog: just show them how.

the keywords

The words used for training I call 'keywords', because they are the key to good behaviour. The pup will also learn from your body posture and body language and, in fact, could manage quite easily without the words if you were consistent with your signals. Humans need words, and most humans fail in their training because they use too many words. This clutters the dog's mental picture and makes it more difficult for it to learn the exact meaning of a single word amongst the many. But the dog is clever and seems to manage to get the gist eventually, despite the failings of its trainer.

Keeping your words and actions simple and clear will speed up your pup's learning, and enhance its ability to take in more of what you want it to do. Once the dog is attuned to learning and has learned to trust you as its trainer, you will find teaching increasingly easy.

The dog can learn to perform an exercise that it already knows on a variety of words, with only a few moments' training to recondition each new keyword. One of my party tricks is to train my dog to take up the sit position on the utterance of any keyword, chosen by a stranger, in less than sixty seconds. Of course the dog I work with is accustomed to learning and he takes his cue from body posture and attitude more than anything, but it looks impressive to the uninitiated!

The actual words do not matter at all. You could train your pup to sit on the keyword 'Bananas' if you wanted to. The dog would be none the wiser. The important thing to the dog is that you show or guide it into the action, attach a word to this action and reward it at the time it is doing the action. The pup will get the message very quickly.

Avoid confusing the dog by using too many words. Many handlers say 'Sit down', when they mean 'Sit'. This is fine until they come to teach the down position and say 'Down'. Imagine the dog's confusion when the same word now means something different! The same goes for 'Get down' to stop the dog jumping up. So does this 'down' word mean 'lie on the floor', 'don't jump up', or 'sit'? Pretty confusing for a human, never mind a dog!

So keep it simple, with one word representing a simple action or even sequence of actions. Eventually you will be able to teach the dog to retrieve on one simple keyword, 'Hold'. This will mean: go out, pick up, come back, sit, give the article and wait – a sequence of manoeuvres all under one keyword. This is pretty advanced stuff, but something to look forward to if you feel like taking it that far. But for now, let us start at the beginning...

motivation

We all work for some gain, although we may be lucky enough to find our work enjoyable. The dog is no different. At the pinnacle of training, the dog should be motivated by the actions themselves, but to start with we need to find something to help motivate the dog into the actions that we require.

There are two basic motivators common to the whole of the animal kingdom (humans included), and these are food and sex. Sex is not an easy tool for humans to utilise in the training of dogs, and more often than not it causes problems! Food is a greater motivator.

essentials of control

We can also use play as a secondary source of motivation because play is the method by which dogs learn to hunt for their main motivation, food. Therefore, play is often an equally good tool of motivation, if not better in some cases.

The art of delivering the correct amount of motivation is a skill that must be worked upon, and you must adjust to your own dog, giving little and often, and learning the point at which to give and the point at which to withhold temptingly in order to induce correct behaviour. If you give too much the dog will see little point in trying; if you give too little it will lose interest. Food or titbits used for motivation should be issued in very small portions. Tiny morsels will keep the pup wanting more for a considerable amount of time, and so extend your training time. If the titbit is too large the dog will take too much time to eat it, and you will lose the momentum of the training exercise.

A tug toy is a safe and durable motivator.

If you are using a toy to motivate your dog, choose something safe and durable, preferably something that you can hold at the same time as your dog, such as a tug toy. You should not teach or allow the dog to run off with the toy as this defeats the object. The fun must be with you, so keep the pup on lead and reel it in when it gets the toy, to enable you to enter back into the game. The toy should not stay in the dog's possession for very long; it must be the dog and not you that lets go of the toy for any length of time. Allow it possession for a few seconds only at a time, and then playfully retrieve the toy from it in such a way that the dog wants to be with you and to play with you.

Play starts off quite gently when the pup is young, but its power will build as it gets physically and mentally stronger, so make sure you maintain control before the play has the chance to turn into a battle.

Just a few basic training exercises will mean that you can control your pup as it grows.

timing

Timing is very important if the dog is to understand what you are trying to achieve. The dog's mind works differently from ours in that it thinks of what is happening to it in the present. This means that it reacts, responds and connects to what is happening *now*. Therefore, whatever the dog has done, it has no idea to what you are referring if you respond even seconds after after the event. It is more likely to connect your words or signals to what is happening at the time you are reacting! Whatever you are trying to achieve (or avoid) should be dealt with as it happens.

After a while the dog learns that a sequence of events leads to a positive result, but this takes time and positive teaching from you so that your dog gets the idea. The more positive and well timed you are, the quicker the dog will learn. So it is important that you are sure of what you are going to do, before you do it, so that you can synchronise things with the exercise.

what to teach

It is essential that the dog understands what we mean by certain words or signals if we are to gain and maintain control as it develops. The earlier it learns to comply readily and happily to these words, the better.

The basic words and/or signals and procedures that the dog needs to understand are: Sit, Down, Stand, Come, Toilet, Leave, Off, Heel, Play, Wait, Bed, That'll Do, Good Boy/Girl, its name, and to be groomed and touched. Some of these words may seem obvious to you. 'Sit', for instance, is probably the first word that most dogs learn. On the other hand, a word that means 'play' might seem a bit odd initially. But if you play with the dog under *your* control, and can turn it on and off when *you* choose, you will gain far better control of the dog, and experience far less problems as the dog's character develops.

essentials of control

For every exercise you wish to train your dog, there is more than one way of teaching it. Some methods are easier than others, and sometimes using a combination of techniques helps you to gain the best control.

where to train

When you first start training your pup, choose an area where you can have some peace and space to concentrate, both for you and the pup. Only when you have mastered a little of the art of control yourself should you attempt to train among the hubbub of the family and other animals. To start with, it is difficult for the pup to concentrate among all the distractions but, once you have gained its confidence and have taught it that working with you is fun, you will find that the distractions do not matter so much.

It is a good idea to attend a good 'puppy play group' or dog training class. These are places for you to learn, for both you and the pup to socialise, and to put into practice what you have been teaching at home (see chapter 18).

when should you start training?

Training should start straight away, irrespective of age, because the pup is learning from you, the environment, and other animals and people around it. Training of a more practical or specific nature can start within a very short time of getting the pup home. Once it has had time to settle in (24–48 hours), you should begin. Do not be tempted to leave the pup much longer, because it is learning all the time – if you leave it to its own devices, you will find very quickly that it is making decisions that do not fit in with your idea of a 'good' dog.

Be consistent about which side you train on.

It is best to train when the dog is alert and lively – not tired, nor feeling uncomfortable from having just eaten, nor needing the toilet. Observe your pup and identify the times when it is naturally active, and choose these times to train and play. Dogs naturally are more active early to mid-evening and early to mid-morning.

chapter seventeen

Remember that the pup's concentration span is not long, so do not expect to keep training sessions going for very long periods of time. It is better to do many short sessions. You can still communicate, play, cuddle and guide it, and intersperse this with control exercise training. However, make sure that your personality or attitude does not change drastically when you switch from play to training. The two are closely related, and both you and the dog should enjoy them equally. The rules of play are just as important as training (see chapter 11). It is a good idea to use the run up to meal times for training; the dog is generally more active, and certainly enthusiastic, at this time, and you can use the food to help with the motivation to comply. In many cases, the first exercise, 'Sit', is trained with the aid of a food dish carefully lifted above the dog's head.

right or left handed

Throughout the training tips and advice, I have instructed you to use a specific hand or arm. This is because, should you want to go on to competition work, the dog will be expected to work on your left (unless you have a disability which restricts this). All the aids and instructions help to encourage your dog towards your left as the working side. If you feel uncomfortable with this, reverse the instructions and it will work just as well. The important thing is that you are consistent, so once you have decided to use your left hand, stick to it. Don't keep changing or the dog will become confused and your training will be less successful.

your voice and hand/body signals

It is a popular misconception that a strong, loud or masterful voice is necessary to train a dog. One of the main excuses for lack of control within a partnership is that the man has a stronger voice than the woman and therefore the dog 'knows that it can get away with things' with the woman. Rubbish! Dogs respond best to a controlled and pleasant voice, they are excited and motivated by an enthusiastic tone (which women are very good at), and only learn to 'get away with things' if this is what the handler allows.

Your voice should be calm, controlled and pleasant at all times. It is not necessary to be loud or dictatorial. Even if you have a very quiet pitch the dog will learn just as easily; its hearing is 16 times as acute as our own, so volume in normal circumstances is not needed. The only time that volume may be necessary is when you are working at a distance with the wind against you, or if the dog has its mind set on something else, but you can then use a whistle to get over this problem (see page 163–164).

Occasionally you may find yourself in a situation which demands an instant reaction because of potential danger for you and/or the dog. At this time a raised, stronger tone will make your dog react more quickly. If it is already used to a louder tone, it is unlikely to detect your note of urgency.

A good way of calming dogs down is to speak to them quietly using a low, soothing tone. Children have a tendency to shriek and have high voices; this excites puppies and even older dogs, and so children should be taught how to talk quietly to the puppy.

Body stance is also important when training your dog. In natural circumstances the dog reads another dog's body posture and knows its state of mind. Just because you are not a dog does not meant that your pup ignores this natural ability. The dog reads a lot from your posture, and therefore taking up a suitable stance will help you to communicate more readily with your pup. Avoid leaning over the dog when you are trying to get it to come towards you, as this will make it defensive and less likely to do what you want. Quite often, it is necessary to come down to its level, so kneel or bend at the knees, keeping your back straight, rather than bending over. If you want the pup to come towards you in a friendly manner, do not lean forward with your upper body and arms, as this will make it defensive, apprehensive and, in some cases, incite aggression. Lean back with arms outstretched, and bring your arms close to your body as the dog approaches.

There *are* times when leaning over the pup is a good idea, as this helps to remind it of your dominance, but this can only be done if the dog is already with you. I must stress that some pups are far more sensitive to body stance and voice than others.

body sensitivity

Different breeds, and indeed individuals within a breed, have differing levels of body sensitivity. A playful pat on the back to a Labrador might feel like a wallop to a similar sized but more sensitive dog such as a Collie. Learn through your play sessions what turns your dog on and off. Get it accustomed to being touched and enjoying it. Some of the more boisterous breeds may well get over-excited by your touch, and you may have to learn when to touch and when it is best to withdraw.

before you start

The most important things to consider before you start are:

- make sure you understand what you are trying to achieve;
- think out how you are going to approach your teaching;
- keep your attitude pleasant, patient and sincere;
- have your rewards ready and waiting, but out of reach of the dog;
- do not blame the dog if things don't go according to plan. The dog is the pupil — a pupil should not take the blame when the teacher (you) makes errors!

To get the best results from training with this book I would advise you to

Get down to the dog's level when you start to train.

Gain your pup's confidence before you start training.

start with the first exercise, even if you feel that your dog can do this already. You will get yourself and the dog into the right frame of mind to continue, and you will understand more fully the techniques and their concepts. (The only change to this is that it might be appropriate to bring toilet training to the top of the list.)

Every dog and every handler is different, so for some exercises I have given more than one technique. For most people, the first choice will be the easiest. I always choose the easiest option – why make things complicated?

Remember If using titbits for rewards, be careful not to create an imbalance in your pup's diet. It is advisable to take the titbits from part of the pup's normal diet, or at least allow for their value when preparing meals.

ending an exercise

At the end of each exercise it is important that the dog knows when you have finished so that it can change position and relax. If it is not sure when you have finished, it will have to make up its own mind, and this will make it *appear* disobedient when it moves out of position at the wrong time! Always tell your pup when to move by using a keyword, 'That'll Do' or 'Finish', and at the same time move the dog from the position or out of the exercise.

If you are just about to end an exercise and the dog finishes or starts to finish before you tell it, put it back in position or take it back to redo the exercise. It is important that the pup learns that you are in control and that it finishes when you say and not when it thinks. It is very tempting for you to follow the dog's lead, especially if you are nearing the end, or losing patience. You are cheating on yourself if you do this, because soon you will have lost the control that you had endeavoured to achieve. Therefore always be sure that you have finished and make sure that the dog is aware of this as well.

essentials of *control*

teaching puppy its name

Teaching your puppy its name might seem a simple task but it is amazing how many puppies respond more readily to words such as 'Dinner', 'Walkies', 'Biscuit', 'Puppy', 'Oi' or, more obscurely, another pet's name, or even a family member's name. The way to teach your pup to respond well to its name is to make good connections with it. The name is there purely as a lever to get the dog's attention and to tell it that we are talking to it and not some other person, dog, animal, or even to ourselves. Therefore the association has to be a good one in order for the pup to be responsive to the next request or direction.

Each time you feed the pup call its name before giving any other instruction. The feeding time routine could go something like this: *'Freddy – Dinner.'* The pup is alerted by the smell and sight of the bowl. *'Freddy – Sit.'* The bowl is raised above the dog's head to help get it into the sit position. If he has done it before, the pup sits eagerly in anticipation of the food. *'Freddy – Eat'* or *'Freddy — Take it.'* The hungry pup needs no more guidance – he complies!

This same principle can be adopted whenever the pup is given food or a reward, or whenever it can see that there is a reward to come. Thus it learns a good and eager response to its own name. Later, even in the absence of the food reward, the dog will turn responsively to see what is wanted.

If the dog is doing something it should not, use its name to get its attention, but you should not get annoyed. Tell it what it *should* do, and reward it when it immediately stops the incorrect behaviour and is good. You must not continue to tell it off for what it had been doing because it will not understand, and will associate your scolding to the new activity it is doing.

If you often use the pup's name in conjunction with chastisement, it will start to go off the idea of responding to it. So be very careful how you use this very useful word if it is to serve you well.

exercise one – **play**

Step one: Find a suitable toy, preferably a tug that you can hold at the same time as the dog. Put the dog on its lead. Go down to the dog's level by sitting or kneeling on the floor. Hold the end of the lead or, better still, trap it under your leg to leave both hands free.

Step two: Encourage the dog to play with the toy. Each time it takes the toy in its mouth, say 'Play', or if you feel that the word needs more emphasis, try 'Get it', or 'Tug'. Choose a word you feel comfortable with, and use it each time the pup takes the article. Repeat the word with enthusiasm while the dog has the toy in its mouth. Anticipate when it is about to let go and stop using the play word.

NB If you wish, once the dog starts to show some ability to do the exercise you can also introduce the appreciation keyword 'Good Girl' (Boy/Puppy/Dog, whatever is appropriate). You may have started already. You should not use this trigger to such an extent that you are in danger of causing confusion or obscuring the importance of the actual keyword that you are trying to teach. In other words, it is very easy to get carried away saying 'Good Puppy' instead of putting emphasis on the keyword. Then when you come to teach the next exercise and its effective word connection, as soon as you say 'Good Puppy', the dog becomes confused, because you have used this word too much in the previously-taught exercise.

Step three: Once the dog is taking the article readily you will be able to identify the times when it is just about to take the toy – at this point introduce your 'play' word. So now you are saying 'play' as the pup is on its way to play. Keep hold of one end of the toy most of the time and do not let the pup run off. Keep it with you by reeling it in on the lead if necessary, but remember you are working on team work, so the pup should not feel pressured. Use a pleasant voice, actions and attitude to convey to the dog your willingness and enthusiasm to work with it.

Always use your chosen keyword to accompany the action. Photograph courtesy of John Barron

Step four: Now you have the dog coming on to the article with enthusiasm, introduce your control a little more by stopping the game whilst it is still very keen. Take the toy out of its mouth (you will probably have to open its mouth physically), move it out of reach and say calmly and firmly, 'That'll do'. Calm the pup with your voice, but not too much.

Step five: Wave the toy in front of it again and, as soon as you see that the dog is keen, say 'Play', and let it take the toy.

Repeat the above steps until you can say 'Play', and the dog will start to play, say 'That'll do', and it stops. As the pup becomes more mature it will be more enthusiastic and play more strongly. You must maintain control of the toys, and not allow the pup to get into the habit of running off with them. Therefore play should be done on lead until you are sure the dog will always return.

exercise two – *the sit*

technique one

With this technique you do not have to manoeuvre the dog with your lead or hands, as the titbit can be used to motivate the dog and lure it into the required position. This is an ideal, and my preferred, technique for all dogs, but is particularly good if your dog is very wriggly or sensitive.

Step one: Arm yourself with a good supply of very small, but tasty titbits. Find a quiet place to train.

Step two: Take control of your dog by putting it on a lead and collar – play with it to get its attention focussed on to you.

Step three: Hold the food in your right hand. Show the dog the food and give it a piece.

Step four: With the titbit in your hand, push your right arm upwards and out. Lift the titbit up above the dog's head and aim slightly backwards so that its head tilts back. Keep aiming slowly back until the dog automatically positions itself in the sit. As it comes into the position say 'Sit', and give the reward straight away. Do not try to keep it in position waiting – this comes later. First the dog must gain an instant reward which it will associate with the action and keyword.

Step five: After the pup has eaten the treat, encourage it to move from the sit by gently pulling it forward with the lead, or clapping to get it to come towards you. As it moves say, 'That'll do.'

Give the treat as soon as the pup is in the correct position.

Follow up: Repeat the exercise as often as you can, but not repetitively; don't bore the dog by doing it over and over again. Two or three times per session is ample. Once the pup is getting the idea, change the position of your body in relation to the pup or choose a different place to do the exercise, so that it realises that you mean the same in differing environments, and also give the titbits only now and again. Do not expect it to understand straight away. When you first change environments, it may feel that you have not taught the dog a thing, but it will not take it long to realise if you follow the steps through and help it all the way.

After a while the dog will start to recognise your right arm movement, and take up the sit position without you saying a thing and, ultimately, you will be able to use this arm movement as a signal for the dog to sit, even from a distance.

Adjust the pup's position until it comes into the sit.

technique two

This technique requires more manipulation of the dog's body, so the handler must be very gentle and yet firm, controlled and sure of his actions. The dog should not be frightened by the handling nor should it feel pressured. It is necessary to restrict the dog's movement somewhat, and use the lead and your hands to execute the position. If you use this method, be sure that the dog is confident about you handling it, and that you feel relaxed manoeuvring it.

Step one: Find a quiet place to train.

Step two: Take control of your dog by putting it on a lead and collar. Play with your dog to get it focussed on to you.

Step three: Hold the lead in your right hand and manoeuvre the dog so that it is on your left or, if it is more comfortable, in front of you.

Step four: Shorten the lead so that you can control the dog with your hands.

Step five: Gently place your left hand on the dog's rump and raise your right hand with the lead slightly up above the dog's head to help angle its body into the sit position. As the dog comes into position say the keyword 'Sit'. Hold it there for a fraction of a second, and then say 'That'll do', as you move it off the spot by gently pulling it out of position.

Follow up as for technique one.

technique three
It is possible and often very successful to use a combination of techniques one and two.

Step one: Find a quiet place to train and arm yourself with some titbits.

Step two: Gain control of the dog by putting it on lead and collar. Have a game to get it in the right frame of mind.

Step three: Have your lead in your right hand, and also a titbit. Shorten up the lead so that you have just 15cm (6in) or so leeway from the dog's collar.

Step four: Place your left hand on the dog's rump and gently push it down towards the sit position. At the same time, hold the titbit between the finger and thumb of your right hand so that the dog can see it. Raise your right hand allowing the dog's nose to follow the titbit. As it reaches the sit position simultaneously release the titbit into its mouth and say 'Sit'.

Step five: Hold the pup in position whilst it eats the titbit, gently releasing the pressure on its rump, but keeping your hand in position in case you need to re-affirm the position. When it has finished the treat, move it out of the position and say, 'That'll do.'

technique four
With a large or leggy breed such as a Great Dane or a Greyhound you could run your hands down the back legs, and gently push in at the back of the knee, at the same time pulling back with the lead or collar, hinging the dog into the sit position. Adopt the same pleasant and controlled attitude towards the dog as above, keep it in position with a titbit above its nose, or by gently holding and soothing with your hands. Finish the exercise as above.

exercise three – *the down*
Teaching the down has many benefits. It is an exercise which teaches the dog that you are dominant over it. It also teaches a high level of control, and is very useful when you want the dog to settle down and keep out of the way for some reason.

technique one
You may find it easier, at least to start with, to bring the dog into the sit position before doing the down, using technique one of the sit. This works for puppies that have sensitive bodies and wriggle under your touch.

Step one: Approach this exercise as you did steps one, two and three of technique one of the sit exercise .

Step two: Bring the titbit down between the dog's two front paws, and hold it there until it flops down. It may take it a while before it tries this position as it may try to paw at your hand to get the food from the stand position, or even get its front end down but keep its back end in the air. Be patient, ignore all this until it comes down and, as soon as it does, release the food reward. Instant release will make it react more quickly next time.

Step three: Repeat as above and, as it comes into the correct position, give the keyword 'Down'. Release the food, a little at a time, as it comes into position, so encouraging it to stay in the down position.

Step four: Once it has finished the treat, release it from the position by gently moving it or clapping to encourage it to move, and say, 'That'll do.'

technique two
This technique works best on calmer puppies.

Bring the titbit down between the dog's front paws.

essentials of control

Step one: Again the dog must be in the correct frame of mind, so play to get it motivated but not over-excited. Place the pup in the sit position using any of the appropriate techniques.

Step two: Once the pup is in the sit, push gently sideways on its shoulder. Once the dog is pushing back at you, change direction. Use your lead to pull in the opposite direction to the one you were pushing in, downward towards the floor and ease the pup down into position. You can push the dog away from you or pull it towards you, whichever is the easiest and most appropriate at the time. The dog will naturally push against you so, especially with larger pups, you can use this to your advantage and adopt the 'martial technique' of taking the dog in the opposite direction to the one in which it is pushing.

Step three: Keep the dog in the down by gently stroking its back, or tummy if it has rolled over. Don't worry about any wriggling, try to keep calm, and keep your stroking soothingly gentle as opposed to quick and exciting.

Use the 'down' when you want your pup to be quiet.

Step four: Keep the pup down for a few moments only, and then gently move it off the spot and say, 'That'll do.'

technique three
This technique works best with the dog starting in the stand position.

Step one: As usual, get control of the dog by putting it on lead, and have a game to get it concentrating on you.

Step two: From the front, place your hands at the top of the dog's legs across the chest and shoulder. Push gently backwards, hinging the dog into the down position.

Step three: Hold the position and finish the exercise by using steps three and four as above.

using the down

Extend this newly-learned keyword and action 'Down' so that you can send the dog to its bed or crate. This is done by putting a reward in the area and encouraging the dog to go to it. Introduce a new word, 'Bed', and control the dog in the area with its lead and the incentive of a titbit or chew. You can also teach the dog to lie down anywhere in the house by taking it on lead and encouraging it to lie down in varying circumstances. A prime time for wanting the dog to be still is while you watch television, listen to music, read or when visitors come. Spend time with the pup on lead showing it what you want in these circumstances. Make sure that it is relatively tired at these times and this will help you to keep the control because the dog will be more happy to conform.

exercise four – *the stand*

Use the titbit to draw your pup ...

The stand has many benefits:

- to stop the dog coming forwards;
- to enable a vet to do a proper examination and take the pup's temperature;
- to keep the pup still while you check it over and/or groom it;
- to stand patiently while being groomed or clipped;
- and last, but not least, if it is to be shown.

technique one

This is suitable for all pups but is especially good for wriggly or excitable animals.

Step one: As with the first technique for 'sit' and 'down', arm yourself with titbits, get the dog on a lead and collar, and choose a quiet place to train.

Step two: Show the dog the food, and then draw the food to the level of the dog's nose and forward, until it comes into the stand position.

essentials of *control*

Step three: As soon as it stands, hold your hand still and let it nibble at the food. Say the key word 'Stand'. If your hand is too high or too low the pup will not come into the stand so adjust your hand position to suit.

Step four: Hold the pup in position until it has finished its reward and then finish the exercise by pulling or encouraging it out of position and saying 'That'll do', as in other exercises.

technique two
Suitable for pups who are happy and very confident to be handled.

Step one: Hold the lead in your right hand close up to the pup's collar, and put your left hand under its body, gently pushing back and up against its back legs to bring it into the stand. Hold it there, talking and reassuring all the time. Repeat the keyword, 'Stand.'

... into the stand.

Step two: Keep the pup in position for a few moments, then release it, saying 'That'll do,' and move it out of position.

technique three
This is suitable for taller or older pups but not for pups that have been abused or kicked at any time. The handler needs to stand upright for this technique.

Step one: Hold the lead in your right hand close to the dog's collar, gently ease your left foot under the dog's body, and slowly and gently raise its body into the stand position. Say 'Stand'. Be careful not to kick the dog; your foot is meant to be a gentle lever, not an instrument of torture!

Step two: Hold the position, leaving your foot on the ground, but underneath the dog's body, and repeat the keyword encouragingly. Keep it there for a few moments only.

Step three: Finish the exercise by taking your foot away, and moving the dog off the spot, using the keyword 'That'll do.'

chapter seventeen

putting the exercises together

If you have adopted **technique one** in each of the 'sit', 'down' and 'stand' exercises, you can now put all three together, using your titbit to draw the dog into position. Learn to manipulate your treats so that you can hold a few in your hand at a time, and keep pushing a fresh one between your finger and thumb. Link the pup's two best positions together first, keeping it in position for moments only, and then drawing it into the second position before it gains its reward.

You will be amazed how soon you can reach this stage. The pup learns quickly with the motivation of food, and the positions are very easy for you to teach once you get used to the correct position your hand should be in to obtain the position required.

It will not be so easy or quick to link actions using any of the other techniques, but you can learn to incorporate the food rewards in all of them and this will speed up the pup's comprehension. Remember, the reward *must* come initially when the dog is first doing and, ultimately, just going into the correct position which it links with the appropriate keyword and signals from you. Later you should randomise the reward so that the pup learns to work with or without it, but always thinking that a reward will come eventually.

using the sit, down, and stand in grooming

It is very important that you groom your dog, not just from a hygiene point of view, but with respect to the social aspect. It is most useful if you can have the dog on a table and teach it that this is acceptable. Even big dogs can be back-breaking when you want to give them a thorough grooming, attend to feet, and so on. Obviously the table must be very stable and strong enough to support your pup when it is fully grown. Some rubber matting or other similar material is a good idea to stop it from slipping. Don't be discouraged if you do not have a table; go ahead with the exercise in the same way. It will be helpful, at least to start with, if someone else can help to hold the dog, particularly a big dog. If not, you will still manage, but you will have to take longer building the dog's confidence. Take time and hold the pup against your body; this is like having an extra pair of hands and will give it extra security. With an older, larger animal that is happy on a lead, it might be beneficial to tie it to something so that you can have both hands free. If you do tie the dog, make sure this does not put it in a position whereby it can fall from the table and damage or even hang itself.

Step one: Collect your titbits and grooming equipment together, and put them within your easy reach. If the dog is on a table, allow it time to sit or lie down to help it gain confidence before asking it to stand. Arm yourself with titbits, and build its confidence by putting a supportive arm around it. When first put on a table most dogs become rather submissive, or a little worried. This is a good time to show that you are in control, and allows the dog to look to you for confidence and reassurance.

Step two: Choose whichever position the dog seems to be happiest in, either the down or the sit. Run your hands over it, let it see the brush and give it a reward.

Step three: Repeat step two and then gently run the brush over the pup in a soothing manner. Talk to it all the time and give a titbit whenever it looks a little worried. Remain in control and do not allow it to become excited. Remember that excitability can be caused by stress, so do not become angry and exasperated — keep your cool and keep control.

Step four: Touch the feet, examine the toes, look inside the mouth, and each time you do something new, back your action with a titbit to show the dog that there is nothing to worry about. Repeat steps one to four until the dog is confident and relaxed.

Step five: Once the dog is stable and confident, raise it into the stand position using your titbit in the right hand, and help it up by placing your left hand under its abdomen and towards the back legs.

Step six: If the pup is new to the table, hold it there and reward, and then allow it to go down or to sit again.

Step seven: If you want to show your pup you will be able to go on from this point, and teach it to stand for the show ring. Even if it is not a breed that is normally shown on a table, it won't do any harm to start there. In fact, it will probably have beneficial effects because you have the dog at eye level and can

'Leave' — prevent the pup from getting the titbit by pulling back on the lead.

control it better. With your gentle reassurance, the pup will learn that this is a nice place to be even though it must remain in a controlled position. Do not allow the sessions to go on for too long, as the pup will soon get frustrated and this will cause you problems.

exercise five - *leave*

This exercise has many applications in the household. Once the pup understands what 'Leave' means, you can show it things you would like it not to touch, introduce the word while maintaining your control, and reward its good behaviour. This is much better than waiting for it to touch things and then scolding it for its ignorance.

It is also necessary to teach the meaning of the word 'Leave' in order to take training further, using the reward-based techniques with the primary techniques explained above.

Step one: Arm yourself with a supply of extra tasty titbits. Take control of your dog on lead, and have a game to get the pup interested in you.

Step two: Bring it into the sit position and show it the food. Give it a piece to taste.

Step three: Offer a second piece, but this time restrict the pup from getting the treat by holding it back with the lead positioned at the back of the head. At the same time, say 'Leave.'

Step four: After a moment, when the pup has relaxed and allowed the lead to be slack, go forward with the titbit, give it to the pup and say 'Take it.'

Step five: Repeat from step two, but this time keep the dog away from the titbit a second or two longer, before you say 'Take it' and allow the reward.

Step six: Repeat from step two, and probably the dog will be starting to get the idea already. Observe its behaviour. If it pulls away from the titbit as you say 'Leave', reward it immediately by giving the treat. This is the behaviour you are looking for — the pup's ability to pull back and not to take unless told to.

Step seven: Increase and vary the time that the pup is left waiting for the titbit, but keep a relaxed hold of the lead, unless you need to use it to stop the pup getting the treat. Wave the titbit around in front of its nose to entice it, but if it reaches forward use the lead to restrain it and say 'Leave.'

Step eight: Build up the time that the pup is expected to wait, bearing in mind that it has a short attention span and, if you leave it too long without a reward, it will think it is not getting anything and lose interest. If it behaves particularly well by turning or moving away, reward it straight away. Vary the time that you prevent it from gaining the reward, so that you do not become too predictable.

Now incorporate your sit, down, and stand exercises and use this 'leave' exercise to help build the time that the dog is held in position. Remember not to do anything for too long, especially when the pup is very young. It is better to be successful than to enter into a battle with the pup.

exercise six – off

Teaching the keyword 'Off' is similar in principle to the 'Leave' exercise. The use of 'Off' is put into practice when you do not want the pup on furniture, or when you do not want it to jump up on yourself or others. There are many times when you will want to use this word, and not always during a training exercise, so adopt the principle whatever you are doing.

Step one: As usual, put the dog on lead and take control. Have a game to gain its confidence and enthusiasm in you.

Step two: Take it to a piece of furniture, preferably one that you do not wish it to get on to. Encourage it to get on to the furniture by patting the seat but, as soon as it goes forward, pull it back with its lead firmly but carefully and gently, at the same time saying 'Off'. As soon as it turns towards you, give a titbit or other reward.

Step three: Try again to see if it will attempt to go on the furniture. Guide it away with your new keyword 'Off', and reward it as soon as it comes away.

Step four: Approach other items that you don't want the dog to jump or climb on and control it in the same manner.

Step five: Set this up with people. Take the dog up to them on its lead in the same manner, and tell it to sit. Control it with the lead and voice, and use your keyword 'Off' before it tries to jump up. Try to identify the time that it might jump and pre-empt it. Repeat the word 'Sit' to tell it

Use a keyword to control when your pup is allowed on the furniture.

what you *do* want. Once it is settled, invite the person to stroke the pup. If it tries to jump ask the person to withdraw until you have gained control.

Step six: If your dog jumps up at *you*, adopt the same technique, using the lead to hold it away from yourself, and incorporating the words 'Off' and 'Sit' to help it to understand what you require. Use your titbit to encourage the sit position. Reward the pup by stroking it and giving a titbit as soon as it is settled in the sit position.

This exercise will be used many times during the dog's learning process and afterwards. Never assume that the dog will understand that it is allowed to do certain things and not others without you teaching it. Even if the pup does not jump on people or furniture at the moment, it is best to teach it the ground rules before it gets into bad habits. It should only go on to furniture if invited, and should *never* jump up at people. You may feel that it is all right for the pup to jump up at you, but this can be taught separately and under your control. Then the dog will jump up only when invited. You will be glad you taught this control when you are dressed up to go out, or perhaps not feeling well. Don't forget the inevitable aspects of the future, when the pup will have grown and be quite large. At some time it is bound to have muddy or wet paws. Your pup will moult, and some dogs do this excessively. You may want to invite friends or acquaintances who are not so 'doggy minded' as you are to your house.

using 'off' to stop the pup following you on to furniture

Step one: Sit down on a settee and, as the pup approaches, say the keyword 'Off', and, if necessary, physically move it off the furniture. Tell it to do something else, 'Sit' or 'Down' or even throw it a toy. Always have a reward ready for good behaviour, and remember that if the pup is not behaving incorrectly then it is being good! Don't be afraid to reward this, even if it is not acting under your instruction. You will probably find it easier to have the pup on lead to give you added control. Be pleasant, controlled and consistent. Keep repeating the exercise until it gets the idea.

Step two: Once the pup has mastered staying off, you can teach it to come up on the furniture with you. Adopt the same procedure: sit on the settee, call the pup to you, tell it to 'Sit', and then show it a titbit on the furniture and say 'Up'. Encourage it up, reward it, allow it a few seconds and then say 'Off', and guide it back to the floor, and reward it again. Repeat this at each training session and, after a while, it will get the idea.

Step three: From now on *never* allow it to come up without invitation. As you see it approach always say 'Off', and make it sit even if you are prepared to let it up. Tell it 'Up' when you are ready. Don't cheat on yourself by allowing it up because you were about to tell it. If this happens, make it stay off, and get the exercise under your control.

exercise seven - coming back (recall)

Teaching the word 'Come' is of paramount importance and is perhaps one of the most important keywords for the dog to understand. It is also one of the exercises most commonly taught incorrectly. If it is not taught correctly to start with, things often go wrong later, when owners find themselves in desperate situations trying to get the dog back to them. For this exercise particularly, a squeaky toy is a great motivator, because it has an audible signal which conveys to the dog that the fun is about to start. You can utilise this later by carrying the toy in your pocket when out for walks, and squeaking it when the dog must come back. This toy should be kept especially for times when you want the dog to come back to you, so that it becomes a special toy, much sought after by the pup because it is not readily available at other times. If your dog is more food oriented, a canister with titbits enclosed will make an audible signal when you shake it and will work equally well.

Step one: Take control of your dog by putting it on the lead and sit with it. Come down to its level, either by sitting on the floor or, with larger pups, on the edge of a chair. If you tower over it, the pup will be defensive and more apprehensive about coming towards you readily. Play with it, and have a toy to encourage it to have fun with you. Also have some titbits ready.

Come down to the pup's level, and play with it.

Step two: Allow the pup to go to the end of the lead in front of you, and then call its name and say the new keyword 'Come'. At the same time, give gentle little jerks on the lead, encouraging it to you. Keep repeating your new word 'Come' in a pleasant, controlled voice, and squeak your toy or rattle your canister. The puppy has no option but to come towards you if you keep jerking and reeling the lead in, but you should make the puppy want to come rather than rely on the lead to do the work. Later, when the pup is off lead, this attitude will be very important. At this point the lead serves only to help guide the dog.

Step three: As soon as the pup is with you, reward it with a small treat and/or game. Coming to you must be a pleasant experience, and you must be very careful that the fun does not stop as soon as the dog gets to you. Keep repeating steps one, two, and three, at different sessions and in various environments, until the dog is happy and confident to come. Give increased rewards as the behaviour gets better.

Step four: Once the dog is coming happily as above, go back to your usual training place (this should be a safe, quiet, enclosed area with few distractions), and allow the dog to be off lead. Arm yourself with a treat and/or toy as before, and allow the dog to wander off within the restricted area. If your training has been very good the pup may take a while to go away from you, but ignore it and wait. Allow the dog a few moments to look at other things, then squeak the toy or rattle the canister and call it back using its name and your keyword. Show it the food and/or toy, encouraging it all the time. Reward with the food and/or toy as soon as the pup is with you. Remember the dog will be less keen to come back if you tower over it, so be aware of your own body posture. Sit on a chair or on the floor, kneel or crouch down. With a very large pup, such as a Great Dane, remain upright but do *not* bend forwards.

If by chance the pup ignores you at this stage, then you have tried to go too fast too soon, your pup has learned an incorrect association, or your reward is not sufficiently motivating. You must start again at the beginning of the training, find a better motivation, and avoid errors. The dog must enjoy your reward more than anything else around it.

Step five: One of the biggest problems in getting the dog to return is that it comes back within arm's length, but you cannot get hold of it to put it back on lead! Keeping good posture will help to eliminate this, but so will this extension to the 'Recall' exercise. Set up everything as in the above stages, but this time when the dog comes to you show it the titbit in your right hand and with your left hand reach forward and touch its collar. Then give the reward and release it with the keyword 'That'll do', allowing it to go away from you again.

Step six: Repeat as above, but this time introduce the 'Sit', as the pup comes to you and before it gets the reward. Use your titbit to bring it into the sit as you did when teaching this exercise earlier. Once again the fun should not stop when the dog gets to you, so have a game and then release it.

When your dog is having fun, you have to persuade it to return. Photograph by Marc Henrie

essentials *of* control

Sometimes the dog comes but sits too far away.

Step seven: Repeat as above, but this time blend steps five and six together, so that when the pup comes to you, tell it 'Sit', using the titbit and then touch its collar and give it the treat.

Step eight: By now the dog is happily coming to you and sitting for the reward. The first time you try this outside your home, choose an area that is as safe as possible, away from other dogs and traffic. Although your training has been thorough, the dog is still an animal, and you must never forget that things can go amiss. Instead of walking off with the dog and expecting it to come back as before, sit down and go through your training. This new environment will be very exciting for a young pup, and it will not understand that its training applies here unless you show it.

Step nine: Stand up but do not start walking. Allow the dog to be distracted and, as soon as this happens, call it back and reward it. Release it again. If there is any hesitation on the dog's part, walk away from it. Call and encourage it to you while still walking away, reward it when it is with you, and have a game. Then release the dog again.

Your pup must be happy to come to you to have its lead put on.

Step ten: Walk a short distance (3–6m or 10–20ft), and call the dog. Reward and then allow it to go again.

Step eleven: Walk a further 3m, call back the pup, reward, put it on the lead and play. Walk a few more paces and release it.

Step twelve: Walk a further 3m, sit down, call it back and play.

What you are now doing is building up an enjoyment in going out for a walk together. A walk should not simply be the dog running ahead sniffing at trees and you following. It should be a team effort, with both partners enjoying each other's company. If the dog learns that the lead going on means the end of its fun, it will always be reluctant to come back. If the dog learns that the fun starts only when it is loose, it will pull you to the park, race off into the distance and think twice about coming back.

If you have already created problems, or your puppy is quite bold, start the training at the beginning, and when you progress to the distance work use a long line to control the dog in the same manner as the lead. Allow the line to drag behind the dog. You have the confidence of instant control, because you can easily catch hold of it. Once the dog is happily coming to you, you can shorten the line, cutting off 30cm or so each time you go out. Eventually, the line will be quite short but by then the dog has developed the habit of coming each time it is called. Do not be in a hurry to take off the line; in fact you may find that attaching the hook and a short length of line will be the way to continue for quite some time, because the dog will always make the desired associations.

Never stop the training for instant recall because, if you allow the dog to start having freedom without being called at intervals, it will become more independent and less likely to come to you when you need it to. Therefore call it back frequently and have fun with it. Even when out for a walk on a lead, call it to you and walk backwards a little, calling it and encouraging it towards you. The more it gets used to doing it, the easier your task will be.

essentials of *control*

If you do lose control, never scold the dog when you eventually get it back, or it will be even less likely to come back to you next time. Simply grit your teeth, smile and resolve to train more thoroughly in future. It does not take us humans long to get things wrong and teach a dog that there is more fun elsewhere, so relax and enjoy your dog, and remember you are a team – work together.

exercise eight --
walking by your side (walking to heel)

To have a dog who will walk on a loose lead, by your side, without pulling your arms from their sockets, must be every dog owner's dream. But for some it is reality!

It is not good for the dog to be allowed to pull into its collar, especially if it has a harsh collar or chain around its neck. Some of the old training techniques, such as giving a good check on the collar or chain to get the dog into the correct position, can actually cause serious damage to the dog's neck. It does not take a very large check to knock the dog's vertebrae out of alignment or cause other similar damage. This type of damage is *not* always easy to spot; how many people do you know who have joint, neck or spinal pains that do not affect their physical appearance? A dog can be the same as humans in this respect, and may react in a similar way, that is, get a bit agitated or grumpy when the pain is playing up but, because it is not limping or showing any other physical signs (and, of course, it cannot tell you), no one can see the pain. Then the unfortunate dog is labelled as having a bad temperament, or as being unpredictable, when really it is just uncomfortable. The only neckwear required is a soft strong collar, with a soft strong lead attached.

To teach a dog to walk by your side takes patience and determination and, above all, a controlled and friendly manner. Starting with a young puppy means that it can learn from the beginning that the only way forward is by your side in a comfortable position for both of you. Incentive forms of training work best in this, as with all of the other exercises, and will help to maintain a bond of trust between you and the dog.

Use a treat to encourage the young pup into the correct position

technique one

Step one: Play with your dog to get it on your 'wave length'. Use your incentive to help create the correct attitude and have your dog on the lead to make sure that it does not wander off or get distracted. Use the lead only as a guide, always work on your relationship being fun and stimulating.

Step two: Manipulate the pup, guiding with your lead and toy or titbit so that it is by your side. Always keep to the same side, at least until it gets the idea. (If you are thinking of doing any competition work in the future, then keep the dog on your left as this is where it should always be worked, unless you have a disability which makes this difficult.) Once it is in position, take a few steps forwards, holding your toy or titbit in position so that the pup follows the incentive. Encourage it verbally, using its name and pleasantries such as 'What have I got?' If the pup is too far forward, encourage it back by holding back the toy or titbit; if it is too far back, use the incentive to encourage it forward.

Step three: Gradually build up the steps until you can walk across your room or garden with the dog in the correct position, that is, by your side on a loose lead, using the toy or titbit as a lure.

Step four: Introduce a word that will mean 'walk by my side' to the dog. Many people use the word 'Heel' or 'Close', but the choice is yours as the dog only understands what you teach. Say the word only as it goes into the correct position, and repeat it while it is doing what you want. It is important that you do not introduce the word until you get the dog where you want it, otherwise it may learn an incorrect association with your chosen word. Remember not to do too much at a time as the pup's concentration span is short, and getting 'walking to heel' correct will make the rest of your life with the dog much more enjoyable.

Step five: Once the dog is happily walking by your side, raise the toy or titbit out of its reach just a little and then give it back. If its attention wanders, attract it back by waving the lure in front of it. Watch its behaviour and learn to give back the reward just before it loses interest.

Step six: If you are patient and do not try to go too fast, the dog will become accustomed to walking by your side, and any other position will not be the norm. Now you can change to another location so that the dog learns to walk by your side in various circumstances.

Step seven: Build up the distance the pup can do very gradually. If you start early with this, before the pup has its inoculations, it will understand quite well by the time it is allowed out. Even so, do not expect great distances from it. As previously mentioned, its attention span is short, but so is its physical ability. Do not put it off by over-walking it the moment it is allowed out safely.

As the dog grows up there will be times when it forgets what it is supposed to do, or something happens to distract it, but you must make sure that you are always aware of what it is doing and guide it into good behaviour.

essentials *of* control

technique two

This technique can be used in conjunction with the above, on its own when the dog is difficult to motivate, or when you have made mistakes with other methods. The way this training technique works is by taking away the opportunity to go forwards, unless it is done in the correct position! We are not introducing any anger, frustration, pain or confusion into the procedure, and the dog is able to learn in a much more positive and favourable manner. If the dog wants to go forward, it will very soon realise how it can be done, and your arms will not suffer in the process.

Sometimes handlers make mistakes in teaching the first technique, and the dog learns to pull instead of walking by their side, because it is striving to get to pleasurable things. As the pup becomes more aware of its surroundings, it sees more pleasure in front of it than it can anticipate from the grumpy person attached to the lead. Ahead it can see fields, freedom, bitches, trees, hamburgers, fun! Looking back up the lead it sees nag, nag, nag, or nag, yank, nag, yank! So who can blame it for pulling away?

Step one: If you have made mistakes, there are many things that must change in you before you can expect the dog to change. First, adjust your attitude. You must be positive and kind. Second, you must perfect your technique and know exactly what you are trying to achieve. Third, you must let the dog know there is a 'new you'. Take it into a room where you would not normally prepare to go out, and place it on a lead and soft collar or harness. Play with it to make sure it is happy with you. Teach it to be on a loose lead before you even start to go forward.

Step two: Get your dog into a sit position by your side. Look down at it and set a mental barrier. Imagine there is a wall immediately in front of your dog's head and it must not walk into it. Now take a step forward. If your dog lunges into your 'wall', guide it back with its lead so that it is walking towards you, take a few steps backwards until it is coming your way and then walk forward again so that the dog passes you going in the opposite direction. Then, because you are holding the lead, the dog will turn to join you by your side. You need say nothing to the dog, unless it is absolutely necessary. A few murmurs of encouragement will do. The main target is for you to perfect this technique. You must prevent the dog from banging its head on your imaginary 'wall'.

Step three: Once you have mastered the technique, you can introduce a keyword that the dog associates with walking by your side on a loose lead. Choose a word that you have not used before, especially if in the past the dog has learned the incorrect associations. A fresh start calls for a fresh word. You could use the word 'Close' or 'Side'; it really does not matter as long as the dog is learning the correct procedure.

Step four: Having chosen the word, put it together with the action by smiling down at the dog as it approaches the correct position, and saying your new keyword. Do not say the word whilst you are bringing it back towards you, only say it when the dog is just coming into or is holding the correct position. If, while the dog is still learning, you use your word in any position but the right one, it may get the incorrect association and then you will have to start again. This is also a good time to offer some titbits to the dog. Have a few in your pocket and hold them down at nose level so that the dog is able to stay in the correct position while it accepts your offering.

Step five: The next step is to train in a different environment. The simplest way is to change rooms or go into the garden. Start from the beginning. Never assume that the dog will pick up where you left off, as this is most unlikely. It needs to learn that you want the same action in this new location. So do not get angry; remember your 'nice head', remember that the dog is a dog and will go into 'auto pilot' unless you show it the correct way once again. In this new area, particularly if there is more space or more attractions, the dog may be more of a handful, but all you need do in this case is over-exaggerate your previous routine. Therefore, instead of taking one or two steps back, make a much more concerted effort and move back with more conviction without, of course, yanking the dog's head off! Continue moving back until the dog is trotting towards you, and then walk forwards again as before. If the dog wants to go off to the side, you must then take the opposite direction. So the rule is, whichever way the dog goes, if it is wrong, you back off, or at the very least walk off, in the opposite direction. Do not allow the dog to pull at any time: you must be ready to react the split second that its head is beyond your mental 'wall'.

Do not have double standards. If you decide the dog must be by your side then *you* must follow this through. Do not assume the dog will 'get it right' in time, particularly if it has been 'getting it wrong' for a while.

Once you have perfected this you can teach your dog to pull, gait (run for the conformation ring), or perform precision heel work. This technique will not spoil any of these, because you are being fair and controlled, and the dog is learning without pressure, which we all know is the best way to learn. The technique will enhance your dog's attitude to working with you and so will have a beneficial effect on its future training, and yours!

exercise nine - *toilet (going when and where you say)*

Toilet training is easy if you accept the dog's limitations, and take note of the fact that given the opportunity it will be clean if it possibly can. The pup's idea of being clean is not to foul its bed or eating areas. Our idea is normally somewhat more refined. Restricting the pup's movement can help to keep it clean (let it sleep and rest in a crate), as can giving it free access to correct areas.

Some breeders are able to give the pups a good start by allowing them a simple means to get out of the bed area and into a suitable toilet area. Many will make a point of calling them to this area when they wake and after feeding. But many will not have the facilities to allow such a perfect start, so the pups may well be used to strolling only a very short distance from the bed before defecating.

Whatever the case, you need to keep a close eye on your pup in order to teach it where you want it to go. The basic idea is to ensure that the dog is in the right place at the right time.

technique one: training to go directly to the toilet area

This is the ideal method because it trains the dog from the start where it must go.

essentials of *control*

Step one: Be aware of your dog's needs and try to anticipate the times when it needs to 'go'. Choose an area of your garden or yard for it to use, away from children's play area or your beloved flowerbed. Decide on a word that means 'go to the toilet', such as 'Toilet'. Avoid any words that might be associated with other exercises, or words that you might be likely to say in other circumstances. Some people choose the phrases 'Be quick' or 'Hurry up', but there are obvious disadvantages to these as you might use them when wanting the dog or waiting for other members of your family. A well-trained dog will try to 'perform' whenever it hears its keyword.

What are you looking at me for?
Photograph by Marc Henrie

Step two: At a time when the pup is most likely to want to defecate or urinate, call it to its special area and wait for it to 'go'. By now you should be able to recognise the signs, that is, sniffing and circling. As soon as it starts to show these signs, encourage it and, as it goes, introduce the keyword. Keep repeating this gently all the time the pup is emptying itself. When it has finished, call it to you and give it a reward. Clear up the mess and wait until next time. It is best not to get into the habit of picking up the pup to take it to the toilet area, as it will have difficulty in learning to make its own way there if you do this and, of course, in the case of a big breed, there is a limit to how long this will be physically possible. Calling the dog to the area and encouraging it to walk there will help it to understand its environment, and realise that there is a specific routine to this toilet business!

Step three: Be aware all the time. The pup may surprise you and need to go more often than you had anticipated. This occurs especially when it first comes to its new home or when there is a change of diet. Each time the pup is allowed to go in the wrong place, irrespective of what you do after the event, it is learning that is the right place to go.

technique two: paper training

This method works well if the pup is accustomed to emptying itself on newspaper perhaps because the breeder has used it in the puppy pen or area. The method is also useful if the pup has to be left for periods of time longer than it can be expected to wait. Having said that, if you are not there to make sure it goes in the right place, the pup cannot be blamed for any mishaps. If you do use this technique, be careful that you do not leave magazines and papers around on the floor. The pup will not know the difference between a paper put out especially for it to use, and one that has been dropped!

Step one: As in all training you must be fully aware of your pup's needs. As in technique one, watch for the signs of the pup needing to 'go'. Place a few sheets of newspaper in a suitably accessible area relatively close to the pup. It is advisable to put a layer of plastic sheeting beneath the newspaper to protect the floor, and prevent any long-lasting odour remaining there.

Step two: When you see signs of the dog needing to 'go', place it on the paper and remain with it, gently keeping it in the area until it has finished. As above, as it starts, give the keyword, and repeat this gently whilst it performs.

Step three: When it has finished, reward it and clean up. Your cleaning must be thorough. Any residue on carpets or flooring will mean that the pup will revisit the spot, whether the paper is there or not.

Step four: Repeat the above steps until the pup is getting it right. Once the pup gets the hang of going to the paper on its own, you can gradually move the paper towards the door and the eventual toilet area. Do not go too quickly or too far, and each time the paper is moved make sure that the pup is aware of where it is. Showing it before it needs to go may not be enough because to begin with it will still look in the previous area, and unless it can see the paper it will be confused and you may be too late.

exercise ten - *waiting its turn*

This is simple to teach if you set your mind to it and are persistent. The easiest way is to work on internal doors in the house first, because there is not so much excitement involved for the pup, and it gives you the chance to get to grips with the technique.

Step one: Put the pup on lead. Set yourself up fairly close to the door, because ultimately you need to go through the door while still maintaining control of the pup's lead at the other side. Hold it back with the lead, and keep relaxing the lead and then tightening it with an upwards movement, until the pup stays back at a given point, in any position it chooses, and then say 'Wait'. As soon as you see it try to keep position, go back and reward it and start again, as this is what you are trying to achieve. Do not push on further without rewarding each stage.

Step two: Once the dog is stable and not trying to pull forward, repeat your key word 'Wait', as you reach forward to open the door a little. You should be holding the lead in an upwards position to control the pup, and repeating your keyword. If the dog lunges towards the door, close it and start again. Be patient. Once the dog keeps its position go back and reward it.

Step three: Keep repeating steps one and two until you can get the door open sufficiently for you to go through. Once at this stage, take a step forward, still controlling the pup by using your lead and voice. Again, if the pup goes forward, go back and make it stay in position. Keep repeating your keyword, 'Wait.'

Step four: Soon you will be able to go through the door but do not allow the dog to move until you are in full control. Keep rewarding good behaviour.

Step five: Once the dog is stable, waiting at the other side of the door, go back and reward it for its good behaviour.

Step six: Now the dog is waiting happily at the other side of the door so call it through and reward it.

Step seven: Start again at step one. You may find that the dog will surge forward straight away again and it is only by repeating the training procedure that it will get the idea.

Step eight: Once the dog is good at all the above, change doors and start again at step one.

Step nine: After each success, change doors until the dog waits at all entrances and exits.

Teach your pup to wait its turn.

Step ten: Incorporate the training without the lead on internal doors to start with so that the pup understands that this is something that must be done both on and off lead.

whistle training

Training your pup to the whistle is no more difficult than teaching it the meaning of words. The beauty of having whistle commands is that they can be heard over long distances and against the wind. A whistle can be heard by a dog over a mile away.

To teach to the whistle all you need do is apply any of the techniques for training exercises and substitute whistle signals for the key words. Of course, if you want your dog to respond for several different actions then you must first teach *yourself* several different sounds and perfect them before attempting to pass them on to the dog. To start with, if the dog has been taught verbal commands, you may find it easier to say the word and then follow it up with the whistle command to help give the dog the idea.

The most versatile of all whistles is the palate or shepherd's whistle, commonly used for sheepdog training. It is possible to get many tones from this whistle, but it takes a lot of practice to utter even a single sound. The palate whistle goes inside your mouth and the air is directed out through a hole in the top part of the whistle. The whistle does not even resemble a whistle but more a bent penny, which is what it was made from originally.

The next best thing, and far more popular and easier to use, is a gundog or plastic whistle. These come in various tones, and can be replaced if necessary by a whistle with an identical sound. They are identified by code numbers printed into each whistle.

Some people like to use other types of whistle and many are fine, but the best option is to go for something that is simple to use and does not require adjustment during training. Traditionally the silent whistle is associated with dog training, but in my experience a more positive sound is better because both dog and handler are hearing the same thing and there is less room for confusion.

The ultimate in a well-trained pet dog – putting away its own toys!

training classes

where to find training classes

The best way to find out about good training classes is to ask around and the best advertisement is recommendation. If you do not know anyone who has been to a good training club, the most usual place to find advertisements is at the veterinary surgery. Often you will see a card or poster on the notice board, and the nurses might be able to help. Local libraries hold lists of clubs that are not run as businesses, and most training clubs and schools advertise in local papers. Local colleges may run adult education evening classes. The Kennel Club holds a list of registered training clubs, and training classes are often advertised in the dog press.

All dogs and owners benefit from good dog classes.

There are various bodies that hold registers of approved and/or qualified instructors. The instructors on these lists are bound by a code of conduct, and they are removed from the list if they break the code. If you do have problems with any instructor, then you can complain to the governing body of which they are a member (see Useful Addresses).

how to choose a good club

Only a few years ago, dog owners would go to a dog club and take whatever the instructor said as 'gospel', attempting to carry out everything that was suggested. The instructor was seen as a kind of doggy 'god', who could do no wrong. Nowadays, people are more aware of what is right and wrong in the treatment of animals, and are increasingly aware that corrective and punishing styles of dog training are neither suitable nor desirable. No one wants to yank their precious pet around on a check chain (paying no heed to the fact that either the dog's vertebrae or its temperament may be damaged), neither would they choose to yell at it if it has not behaved as they would like. However, at one time that attitude was prevalent in many dog clubs. Some clubs would go further and issue rolled-up newspapers or even pincher collars to possible problem cases or even as a matter of course! Then you would be told to 'praise the dog' afterwards, as if this would magically make it all right. Of course some clubs proved the exception to this rule, but if this is how you remember dog training, cheer up, there is a band of new crusaders who believe there is a better way for you and your puppy.

Animal behaviour is not a new science but, on the whole, dog trainers have been slow to use the available knowledge to design training methods suitable for all types of dogs and their owners. Reward and motivation have now become the norm, and aggression and a stern attitude are out of date. This does not mean that dogs should be allowed to run amok ; in the experimental stages, some dog trainers tended to have classes akin to a slapstick bunfight! It is important to maintain control at all times.

The good dog club has a controlled and happy atmosphere. The dogs are not running around unattended, nor are they unduly restricted and harassed. Dogs are on lead unless the instructor asks for them to be free. You may see a

The class should have a calm and pleasant atmosphere.

handler sitting on the floor with the young dog, or crouched by its side to give confidence. Definitely you will see toys or titbits around. A dog and handler will not be left with a problem and be expected to sort it out without help. You will not see the dogs and handlers marching around the hall, robot fashion. You will not find a handler who has been coming for years and still has an uncontrollable dog. The instructor's own dogs will obviously enjoy being with him, and the dogs will not be apprehensive while working. There should be no yelling and screaming.

The best advice I can give is that you start early, before your pup is through its inoculations. Find as many names and contacts as you can and then go along, without your dog, and watch for an evening or two. It will soon be obvious what methods are used and whether the dogs and handlers are happy, contented and controlled. This is not to say that every dog will behave impeccably – after all, they are there to learn. However, like people, dogs should be taught to walk away from trouble. They should be given an alternative form of behaviour, and handlers should not scold every time the dog misbehaves and then watch

chapter eighteen

A puppy class is a good place to socialise.

for the next wrong move. For example, if the dog has a problem with the Labrador next to it, then it should be taught that it is more fun to be occupied with a toy, a titbit or its owner than to beat up its neighbour. Owners are taught to observe and recognise signals in their dogs, and to anticipate and prevent incorrect behaviour rather than watch the dog go wrong. If the dog makes the same error continually, it is learning that this mistake is all right, no matter what the handler does after the event.

puppy classes

Some training schools have special puppy classes, and one of these can be a very good starting point for you and your pup. Normally puppy classes have an upper age limit of about five months, depending on the maturity of the breed, and numbers are limited from around five to ten, so you and your puppy will receive the best attention.

You will be encouraged to train your pup using many of the methods in chapter 17. Puppies are taught how to play with other pups and come back to you when you call, using the play as a reward. This means the pup is allowed to play, comes back for a titbit or toy, and then goes back, when told, to play. Thus the whole experience is pleasant, and the dog does not strive only to play with the other dogs and not with you. During the time when the pup is by your side and you are listening to your instructor or watching the others, your pup is learning to lie beside you in a controlled manner. This is a good exercise to use at home and will help you to watch your favourite television programmes in peace and not be pestered by your pup. Many schools encourage multi-handling, that is, your pup is handled by other people in the class and you will be able to handle other people's pups. This helps the pup to enjoy and not be fearful of other people's attention, and lessens its dependence on you. It is a great experience for all.

training classes

club activities

Clubs and training schools vary in what they have to offer. This normally depends on the structure of the club, the number of people involved and, of course, the time that they can devote to it.

The traditional structure is that of a group of people giving up their spare time, mostly for little or no financial gain, to help others achieve the control that they have with their own dogs. Other clubs or schools are organised on a more business-like basis with one or two professional instructors who make part, if not all, their income from dog training. The third structure involves local county councils and/or colleges which employ instructors to teach dog training at adult education classes. No one type of club is better than the others. It really does depend upon the individuals involved, and there will be regional variations on all of the above.

Some clubs run their own ladder to success in the form of regular tests and competitions to encourage you to work hard on your training. The Kennel Club has organised a scheme called the Good Citizen Test. This involves basic obedience exercises geared towards good control in the day-to-day life with your dog, and many clubs and training groups now teach pupils to work towards attaining this level of competence.

Many clubs will teach you how to train your dog for various disciplines once you have gained basic control. The most popular of these are Agility, Ringcraft (showing your breed for conformation), and Competitive Obedience. Clubs may also cover more specialised sports such as Flyball, Working Trials, Gundog work and Water Trials, but if you want to progress to these activities, you may need to find a specialist trainer or club. Some clubs even have display teams, and you can work towards being a member if you wish.

There are many activities that you and your pet can enjoy together. Photograph by Pam Martins

health and hereditary diseases

Recognising when your pup is off colour is part of being an attentive owner. Little things will tell you if your pup is unwell. Often the first sign is lack of appetite, followed by lethargy, or quite simply a change in its normal character. Getting to know your pup, its body, and its little ways in intimate detail will help you to take action early. This can sometimes help to eradicate problems, or at least make an early detection of ill health which may even save your pet's life.

Sometimes you will know that there is something not quite right with your pet, and yet it will be difficult to say just what it is. Monitor its behaviour and keep a record of any changes. Do not be afraid to take it to the veterinary surgeon for a check up straight away if you are concerned. Even if the vet can find nothing amiss at that point, there is a record of your observations which, if something underlying is wrong, it will help in a future diagnosis. Just as with humans, some illness are very difficult to detect or diagnose. What makes things more difficult is the animal's inability to speak our language, so you must learn to understand your pup's language. It speaks it with its body, attitude, behaviour, character and eyes.

Small upsets can be treated at home sometimes, and minor ailments will clear up with a little basic first aid or medication. But you must be very careful when treating illnesses yourself as simple problems may be the outward signs of something more complex, so if you are at all unsure you should seek veterinary advice immediately. I usually use the rule; if this were my baby would I take him to the doctor? If the answer is yes, then it's off to the vet.

common parasites

Fleas

Probably the most common and most talked about parasite is the humble flea. Surprisingly, the cat flea is the one most usually found on dogs. The fleas land on your pet and indulge in an orgy of food and sex until they die of exhaustion about a week later. They feed on your dog's blood. They lay their eggs on the dog but these fall to the ground, into your carpet, into cracks and crevices, or into the dog's bedding, and there they stay until a couple of days later when they hatch. Therefore simply spraying your pet is not good enough to eradicate the pest. The larvae feed on organic debris for a week or so, and then spin a cocoon. The pupae hatch anything from five days to several months later depending on the conditions, and then seek out a host so the cycle starts again. The pupae are almost impossible to spot, and can take on the appearance of whatever environment they are in. Each adult female is capable of laying 500 eggs!

health and hereditary *diseases*

There are various products available that break this life cycle. They are based on flea hormones and contain a growth regulator which prevents the young developing into adults. Some dogs have a flea allergy and extra care must be taken to prevent infestation, especially in the summer when fleas are most prevalent.

Check your dog for ticks after you have been for a walk in the country.
Bullmastiff photograph courtesy of Cheryl Gillmore

Ticks

Ticks are another common problem, especially for those who live in, or are regular visitors to, the countryside. There are several types, but the most common ones that attack dogs are the sheep tick and the hedgehog tick. Ticks are most prevalent in grassland, scrub and woodland. They normally live on cattle, sheep, goats, deer, rodents and, of course, dogs and cats, but they also attach themselves to humans.

At first, all you will see is a greyish swelling attached to the animal. Close inspection reveals the legs, but the head will be buried in the animal's flesh.

Left alone, the tick will gulp the blood of its host for days before dropping off. There are many sprays available that guard against ticks, and prevention is better than cure. If your pup, or you for that matter, do get 'spiked' by the tick, do *not* try to pull it off as you may only remove the body, leaving the mouth parts to fester in the skin. Some people use a lighted cigarette to burn the tick which makes it let go, but this can be dangerous, especially with a wriggly puppy. The best solution is to dab cotton wool soaked in alcohol, ether or acetone (nail polish remover), on the offender. A small, commercially-produced tool is available that lifts off the tick.

chapter nineteen

Mites

There are several different types of mite: some burrow into the skin, others live on the surface. If allowed, they live their entire life on their host. All mites cause dermatitis, sometimes itchy, sometimes not, depending on the type of mite.

Often the first signs are increased scratching or hair loss around the tips of the ears. If left untreated, this spreads and the areas may become thickened or inflamed. Some of this is due to the mite and some due to the animal's own scratching. Some mites such as *Sarcoptes* can cause scabies in humans so it is important that the matter is attended to straight away. *Sarcoptes scabiei* is the mite that most commonly causes mange. Suspect this if you see red patches under armpits and on the inside of the thighs. Often it causes bare patches around the eyes and ear flaps. If the condition is not treated it will spread quickly around the body, forming scabs, sores, and bare patches throughout the coat. Puppies and young children are most susceptible because their skin is soft, but nobody is safe!

The mite *Cheyletiella* causes a condition often referred to as 'walking dandruff', because it causes the production of excess scale. Mites can move on to humans but do not live very long. This condition can be treated with insecticidal shampoo (some vets even recommend human anti-dandruff shampoo).

Dermodectic or follicular mange is caused by *Demodex canis*. This tends to be more common in smooth-coated breeds. It causes the coat to go dry and scaly, and the skin becomes thickened and wrinkled. There is a 'mousy' smell. If untreated, a bacterial infection will take hold and the dog may die. It is normally transmitted by a mother to her young, and is not easily transmitted to adult animals. It is very difficult to treat, and veterinary assistance is essential.

Otodectes cynotis is the ear mite that lives in the ear canal. The first signs of this are increased rubbing and scratching of the ear, and excess dark-brown, waxy discharge. Sometimes you can see the mites, which look like small, white moving dots. It is possible that a grass seed caught in the ear or other infection can cause the same sort of reaction in your dog, so it is always best to check with your vet and receive the correct treatment for your pup.

Worms

As soon as you get your puppy, check up on worming, firstly by finding out what your breeder has already done and secondly by getting veterinary advice on what to do from then on. It is very important that your pet is protected against major infestation, and that any worms already in its system are eradicated or controlled.

Round worms (*Toxocara canis*) are the most common and most talked-about worms in dogs. These are large fleshy worms; careful control is of paramount importance.

Pups can be affected even before birth by larvae that pass from the bitch's muscles to the uterus after the 42nd day of pregnancy. The larvae make their way through the liver and lungs and eventually into the small intestine of the pup. By the time that the pup is about three weeks old the worms are fully developed into adults. On top of this, the pup can receive further infection from the mother in the form of larvae in her milk. This creates a heavy burden on the pup's system, and may stunt its growth. You may see a distended stomach, and the pup may vomit or have diarrhoea. In very severe cases, the intestine can become blocked. Pups start to expel the worms at approximately seven weeks of age, and by the time that they are seven months the adult worms are mostly gone. However, the pup will probably ingest some larvae, which will go into a state of rest. Adult dogs pass large amounts of worm eggs: several thousand can be found in a minute amount of faeces. The egg is very resilient, and in ideal conditions will rest for about 14 days while the larvae is developing inside. The larvae stays inside the egg until it is eaten by an animal, and can survive for as long as two years waiting for a host. If ingested by humans (usually children), in most cases the larvae make their way through the body with no ill effects. Very occasionally they find their way into the eye, which may cause an infection, but I must stress this is very rare.

If the larvae finds itself in a bitch it will rest until she becomes pregnant, and then most will migrate to infect her puppies. Some will remain, to infect future litters.

Tape worms, which can grow up to 50cm (20in) long, attach themselves to the intestine of their host, and are often not detected until segments are passed by the animal. The immediate host for the *Dipylidium caninum* tapeworm, which is the most common, is the flea.

Ring worm is recognised typically by round areas of pink, inflamed skin, with crusty edges. Sometimes there will be just irregular bare patches, anywhere in the dog's coat. Ringworm is extremely contagious, not only to other animals but also to humans, especially children. Ringworm is actually caused by a fungus, and spores can live away from a host on trees, gates and upholstery for several years.

Hook worms are stout, short worms with characteristic hooked heads. These worms attach their mouth parts to the intestinal mucosa, damage the surface and then eat the damaged material. They can cause loss of weight and anaemia. Larvae may penetrate the skin and cause dermatitis.

There are obviously many more parasites, but these are the most common. Always seek veterinary advice if you suspect any infestation, and take precautions by protecting your pet with relevant medication as instructed by your vet.

infectious diseases

You can inoculate against most of the life-threatening diseases, and one of the first things you will do with your pet is to visit the vet to ensure that your puppy is fully protected.

Distemper

Distemper can occur in two ways: the first is very mild and in many cases will not even be detected. The pup may go off its food and may be depressed. Recovery is good and often the pup is on the mend before you realise it is ill. The more important condition is 'acute distemper'. The dog has loss of appetite, persistent depression, raised temperature, fever, throat infections, a dry cough, discharge from eyes, dehydration, vomiting, diarrhoea and hard, painful nose and pads. Immediate veterinary advice and treatment is required.

Distemper is most common in uninoculated puppies and dogs who have lost their immunity. It is passed in bodily fluids and is also airborne, and therefore can be transmitted without any physical contact. It is controlled by inoculation which can be given from around six to eight weeks for a primary inoculation, followed by a second at around twelve weeks of age to complete the protection.

Canine Leptospirosis

Leptospirosis is caused by a bacterium called a *spirochete*. The organism is spread by contaminated urine which recovered animals can excrete for up to a year. Rats and cattle, as well as other dogs can pass the disease (sometimes known as *Weils disease*), and humans are also susceptible to it. The bacteria enters the body through breaks in the skin or mucous membrane, through ingestion, and occasionally through breeding.

In its worst form, it causes sudden death in young puppies, which often have no previous signs of ill-health. The secondary type shows itself by the pup becoming jaundiced, depressed, feverish, followed by vomiting, diarrhoea with haemorrhages, dehydration, shock, and death within a few hours. The third type makes the dog feverish, depressed, it will vomit and the kidneys swell, causing pain. Halitosis and oral ulceration occur. The final type is very minor and often is not diagnosed. It involves fever, depression and lethargy lasting only a few days.

Vaccines are available to prevent this disease and these will be included in your inoculation package. Annual boosting is essential because immunity is short lived.

Canine Parvovirus

This can cause sudden death in puppies, which show signs of heart failure. Signs are: vomiting, which degenerates to bile or blood-stained fluid; profuse diarrhoea, of a very liquid red/brown colour, and foul-smelling; rapid dehydration, and shock. Death will occur in a very short time if untreated. Once again this disease is now preventable by inoculation.

Infectious Canine Hepatitis (ICH)

In its worst form, this can cause sudden death in newly-born puppies. They may be off their food for a short while, and occasionally cry prior to death because of abdominal pain. In the acute form, dogs become depressed, feverish, and have pale or jaundiced mucus membranes. They have abdominal pain, throat infections, and may pass diarrhoea with blood in it. They may appear tucked up and reluctant to move. They may cry due to the abdominal pain before they die. The sub-acute form is recognised by depression, loss of appetite, and corneal oedema or 'blue eye'. The virus is excreted in the faeces, urine and saliva, and may continue to be secreted up to six months after the dog has recovered.

Kennel Cough

Kennel Cough, also known as Canine Cough or Canine Bordertella, is caused by inhalation of micro-organisms, and gives the dog a dry cough. Often it sounds as though something is stuck in the dog's throat. Sometimes there may be a nasal discharge, but generally the dog remains bright and active. Often the dog starts to cough if it becomes excited. Kennel Cough is contracted when dogs are kept in close proximity, or are breathing the same air. The micro-organisms invade and colonise the respiratory system. It is viral, like the common cold, so there is no treatment but vets often treat the dog with antibiotics to prevent secondary bacterial infection. Sometimes, if the cough is particularly troublesome, an expectorant cough medicine can be given to help loosen the mucus.

health and hereditary diseases

If every dog were inoculated, many diseases would not be as common as they are at present.
Photograph by Marc Henri

The incubation period (the time it takes for the cough to take hold after the dog has come into contact with it), can be as short as three days, but more commonly five to seven days pass before any symptoms show. The cough can be persistent and last two to three weeks, but many dogs get over it within a few days. When the dog stops coughing it can carry the infection and pass it on to others for up to 12 weeks.

There are vaccines available against some of the strains, for instance *Bordertella bronchiseptica,* which is boosted six monthly and given intra-nasally, and *parainfluenza* which can be included in the annual booster.

Because of its name, owners often believe that this problem is contracted only in a kennels environment. In fact, whenever dogs come together, and especially if they are breathing the same air in an enclosed area, they are at risk if an infected dog or a carrier is present. The bacteria particularly like damp, humid conditions and multiply rapidly in these circumstances.

Rabies

The rabies virus can infect any warm-blooded animal, including humans. The disease enters the body through a break in the skin, or through the mucous membranes. It is most often passed from the saliva into a wound, following a bite from an infected animal. It affects the nervous system, and causes behaviour changes, but signs are variable and this makes diagnosis difficult to begin with. Some of the common behaviours displayed are: over-protectiveness, shyness, apprehensiveness, insecurity, restlessness, biting at moving or imaginary objects. There is a change in the animal's voice as its vocal chords become partially paralysed. Sometimes convulsions cause death. The animal cannot ingest food or water and so becomes dehydrated, its mouth hangs open and saliva drips from it. Eventually the animal becomes totally paralysed and dies.

Rabies is not common in every country in the world and some authorities of 'rabies free' countries operate a quarantine system for animals who are to be moved from country to country. Others operate a health passport regime. You should have your dog vaccinated if you live in a country where rabies is a problem, or if the dog is to be moved to an affected area.

common hereditary defects

There are many hereditary defects, and almost every breed has some that affect it. There are commonly-used tests for some of the defects, and sometimes scoring schemes to give you an idea of how bad the defects are. Understanding these will help you to ask the right questions when purchasing a puppy. Furthermore, if you decide to breed from your pup, you need to understand the procedures and how to tell if your chosen stud dog or brood bitch is a suitable match for your dog. Some of the more common problems are given below, but consult experienced breeders and your vet to help with hereditary problems specific to your breed.

Hip Dysplasia

This is a polygenic problem, which means that it is inherited as a result of the influence of several genes. It shows itself as an abnormally shallow acetabulum and small or mis-shapen femoral head. It is not always easy to outwardly detect Hip Dysplasia, often referred to as HD, although sometimes owners and/or vets are suspicious when the dog starts to limp on its hind legs, particularly if the breed is prone to it. Radiographs (X-rays) are needed of the hips to make a diagnosis and examine the severity of the condition.

The British Veterinary Association (BVA) and The Kennel Club run a scheme to detect and score the severity of HD. It is not possible to score your dog for HD until it is at least twelve months old, although vets sometimes take X-rays earlier if they suspect a severe problem. If you have a breed that is routinely screened for HD, or you think your dog may have it, find a vet who specialises in the subject. Your local German Shepherd Dog club, or a club of another breed known to suffer from the problem, can give you the name of a suitable vet.

Your dog will probably need to be X-rayed under an anaesthetic, and there is always a slight risk with any anaesthetic. If you use a vet who is an expert in taking X-rays for HD, then you minimise the chance of the X-rays being rejected as unreadable. You need to take along your Kennel Club registration certificate for identification purposes. The X-ray plates are then sent by your vet to the BVA panel of scrutineers for scoring. The lowest score per hip is 0, the highest possible is 53. Therefore a perfect hip score would be 0:0, and the worst 53:53.

Each breed has a breed average, which is a mean of both hips, and this average is adjusted regularly as more scores are taken into account. Your vet will be able to give you a copy of the breeds and their scores. If you wish to help eradicate or control the defect you should only breed from animals with a below–average score. Results are published by The Kennel Club in *Kennel Gazette*.

Osteochondritis Dissecans

Better known as OCD, this is a malformation of the cartilage, especially between the femur and humerus. Like HD this is a polygenic defect. If your pet is limping and in obvious pain you should suspect this defect, which can be confirmed by X-ray. An operation performed by a specialist vet often helps to relieve the condition. Do not breed from animals with this condition.

health and hereditary *diseases*

Eye Defects

There are many eye defects with various genetic origins. The BVA/Kennel Club/International Sheepdog Society monitor inherited ocular disease. Different diseases are detectable at different ages, and dogs are examined by a member of the eye scheme panel and not by your own vet. Your vet will be glad to refer you to your nearest tester.

In breeds where problems are common or suspected, it is recommended that the test is done every year. It is unnecessary to give an anaesthetic, but the examiner does need to put drops in the dog's eye, which have to be allowed to take effect to permit a good examination of the eye. Your dog may be a little worried by the experience, as the examiner must get very close to its face and the room is darkened, but most testers take the time to make friends with the dog before starting. A list of common eye defects is as follows:

- Central Progressive Retinal Atrophy (CPRA) and Generalised Progressive Retinal Atrophy (GPRA). Both of these are often referred to simply as PRA.
- Hereditary cataract (HC).
- Primary Lens Luxation (PLL).
- Gonodysgenesis/primary glaucoma.
- Collie eye anomaly (CEA).
- Retinal dysplasia (RD).
- Persistent pupillary membrane (PPM).
- Congenital cataract (CHC).
- Persistent hyperplastic primary vitreous (PHPV).

Other common defects associated with the eye, which can be seen without testing, are Entropian, which is inward turning of the eyelid, and Ectropian, which is outward turning of the eyelid. Entropian and Ectropian can be surgically rectified, but affected animals should not be used for breeding.

Umbilical Hernia

This shows itself as a protrusion of tissue coming through the umbilical ring. There is no testing for this condition as it is quite obvious. You should avoid using stock carrying this defect but in some breeds it is not regarded as a major defect, so breeding with affected animals continues. This is so especially where the gene pool is small, and is also the case with numerically small or rare breeds. Umbilical hernias are often left because they do not normally cause any problem to the dog, although unusually large ones may have a tendency to be caught on undergrowth. If an animal is to be bred the hernia may be surgically repaired prior to the mating, because of the extra pressure on the animal's abdomen when carrying young.

Haemophilia

This is a failure of the clotting mechanism of blood. There are many different types of haemophilia which occur due to differing abnormalities. Haemophilia A (factor V11 deficiency) is the most common, and is sex-linked.

responsible dog
ownership

As the owner of a new puppy, you have responsibilities to your pet, to your family and to the public. You must always make sure that your pup has all its needs taken care of. Care and control of your pet are of paramount importance.

identification

Your pup should, both by law and by good sense, be identifiable by means of a tag attached to its collar, which gives your name, address, and a phone number if possible. You may add your dog's name if you wish, but it is more important that your name is included to ensure your

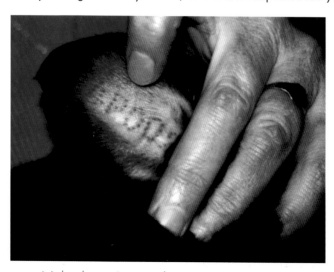

A Labrador pup's tattooed ear.

pet's safe return. Various other methods of identification are available, including tattooing and micro-chipping. Neither of these methods are mandatory in the United Kingdom as yet, but it is a good idea to use one of these more permanent means of identification to protect your pet. It is possible that the collar gets broken or the identity disc lost, and then your pet cannot be identified unless it is marked by another means.

If you are on holiday with your pet, make sure that you put your holiday address as well as your home address on the tag.

hygiene

Always clean up after your dog, both at home and when you are in a public place. Many councils provide bins for dog faeces, and you should always carry a 'pooper scooper' or a plastic bag to pick up after your dog has defecated. If you are using bags, try to make sure that they are biodegradable, otherwise we get rid of one problem and create another. If you cannot find a suitable place to put your bag, then I'm afraid you must take it home. The local and national laws do change with regard to the disposal of faeces, so check your by-laws with your local environmental health officer.

responsible *dog* *ownership*

control

Your dog comes under the dog laws as set down nationally and locally. Each area has its own by-laws that you must obey, and your local dog warden will be able to help you with your dog and the law. Essentially, you are totally responsible for your dog, and any other dog that you handle. Therefore you must maintain complete control all the time. If someone feels frightened or threatened by your dog, even if they are not bitten or attacked, they have grounds for complaint. At worst, this may result in your dog being destroyed (and this does happen to what might seem the most innocent of dogs), or at best your dog is placed under a strict restraint order. Even if the dog is on your own premises it must be under control. In Great Britain a guard dog must have a handler with it at all times.

The laws may be different in other countries, and are constantly being revised, so you should always check with the relevant official bodies to be sure of your rights and those of your dog.

Never allow your dog to run free amongst or near livestock. You may believe that your dog is completely safe, but you may be putting the other animals under stress, and many dogs cannot resist giving chase if livestock start to run. Farmers are entitled to shoot first and ask questions later if they think that a dog is threatening their animals.

Apart from the law, you have a moral duty to control your dog, and not to cause fear in others. It can be daunting for a member of the public to see even a relatively small dog running towards him. If that person is with his dog, he will fear for himself and his pet. This will make him tense, which will be immediately and uncontrollably passed on to his dog, who will respond in dog fashion by going on the alert. In turn, this will alarm your dog which will observe the alert body posture and attitude of the other and go on guard in its turn. Even if neither dog is normally considered a fighter, the result could be a fight, or at least an upsetting disturbance. Each owner will blame the other, and a situation develops just because you did not have the courtesy to keep control of your dog. Your pet will now expect other dogs to be antisocial and, unwittingly, you have created a dog that goes looking for a fight. You will also have created a problem for the other owner, whose own dog now expects that approaching dogs are ready to fight, so it may bark and try to 'have a go'. Another aspect is that you never know what that other dog's temperament is going to be like, and therefore it is foolhardy to risk your dog getting bitten.

If your dog is running free in a public area, you should always make absolutely sure that you can get it back to you, whatever the circumstances. Never let it go too far, and always call it back before it has a chance to go off investigating other dogs, animals or people.

If you are in any doubt at all, keep your dog on a lead. You and your dog will have just as much fun as long as you have built up a bond and your training has been thorough. Release it only when you know the danger has passed.

Some councils may restrict you to keeping your dog on lead, especially on main roads and in parks with children's play areas or sports fields. There may be restrictions or even a total ban on dogs on beaches. Some councils have created a fenced-in area for dogs only. Here you can allow your dog to defecate, and often facilities are provided for cleaning up. Many shops and most cafés and restaurants have bans on pets due to hygiene regulations. Make sure you are aware of where you can and cannot take your pet. If you are going out for the day with your dog, make sure that your destination will allow, or is suitable for, your dog. If not, you must provide adequate facilities for it to be left behind. You cannot leave your dog in a car in hot weather for even a short period. The car acts as an oven, and the dog will soon be baked alive. Even in cooler weather, always leave windows open for ventilation, put down fresh water, and cover areas where the sun might come in.

Keep up your training so that when you are out in a public place your dog is something to be proud of. A well-trained dog turns heads and makes you friends. A neglected dog will only make you enemies.

neutering your dog

It is now considered very acceptable to have your dog or bitch neutered. This means the surgical removal of a dog's testicles or a bitch's ovaries and uterus under general anaesthetic. It is increasingly popular to neuter at an early age to prevent unwanted puppies in the bitch and behavioural problems in the dog.

If you have no intentions of breeding, then it makes sense to give the operation serious consideration. For the bitch, apart from unwanted puppies, it prevents the regular seasons of oestrus (heat) and, consequently, the unwanted attention of males, and can also help to prevent medical problems in later life. Entire females are more prone to conditions such as pyometra and mammary carcinoma.

Most veterinary surgeons want to spay a bitch about eight weeks after a season, but it is not a good idea to carry out the operation while the bitch is pregnant or having a false pregnancy. To give the bitch the best benefits, the operation should be carried out when she is young, and you should speak to your vet to help you to find the optimum time.

There are even more benefits for the male, because castration can have a marked effect on behaviours that can be troublesome to the pet owner or trainer who wants to work with the dog. An entire dog is more prone to conditions such as enlargement of the prostate gland and testicular tumours.

Some dogs are born with the condition *cryptorchidism*, which means the testicles do not drop into the scrotum (this should have happened by the time the dog is about 10 months). The cryptorchid dog is prone to tumours in later life. Other dogs can be *monorchid*, which means only one testicle has descended. These conditions are hereditary and you should not breed from dogs who have either of these conditions.

For those males who develop problems in their behaviour, castration, particularly early castration, can help to control if not eradicate *some* problem behaviours. If you are considering castration because of behavioural problems, it is almost certain that you will need to follow a programme of behavioural modification (training) to help the dog adjust. Although its behaviour may have been exaggerated by the amount of testosterone in its body, this attitude will also fall into the category of learnt behaviour, and so needs to be 'unlearned' or 'reconditioned'.

The age at which the young male is best castrated is just after he learns to cock his leg, at the onset of puberty. This is the time that the Guide Dogs for the Blind Association castrate their young males, and it has proved to be the optimum time to prevent behavioural problems.

People often worry about castrating a dog when they do not think twice about spaying a female. It is often men who find it most difficult to accept. The dog does not think in the same way that we do, and leaving a dog 'intact' will cause him far more mental and even physical trauma than allowing the reduced drive that castration gives. There is no benefit in allowing 'just one bitch', because this will certainly not calm him down. In fact, it could have just the opposite effect.

Dogs who have not been castrated are more likely to fight with other male dogs, more likely to elicit aggressive behaviour from other dogs, and more likely to urinate in the house, especially if another dog has been there. They may be more dominant and aggressive over possessions, and prone to roam, especially when smelling a bitch on heat.

In the wild, wolves only come 'on heat' once in the early part of the year. Domestic dogs have two seasons and these can be at any time, so the entire male dog is frustrated and may be off his food many times a year. Together with with the desire to become a father, this could trigger many of the behaviours that are undesirable in a domestic situation.

On the down side of castration, occasionally the coat can be affected, slightly changing its texture. There is also the possibility that your castrated male may smell a little like a bitch to other dogs, and this confusion can be heightened by a bitch being on heat nearby. But this causes far less problems to the animal than it would if he was an entire male.

Castrated males are often said to put on weight, but this is a misconception. Most dogs do not need as much food after they have had the surgery, because they are no longer burning up calories chasing females. Also their appetite may be a little better following the operation, because they are less anxious to find a mate, and food is the next most important motivator.

Owners are tempted into feeding more, because the dog now has a good appetite. Therefore it is the food increase that causes weight gain, not castration.

The same applies for bitches. Reduced sexual activity lessens the need for nutrition, and therefore owners must monitor weight gain and food intake to maintain good condition.

in conclusion

I hope that you have enjoyed reading this book, and that it has helped you to understand your new pup. You now have a better chance of enjoying the company of your pet for many years to come, knowing that you are doing all you can to makes its life happy and fulfilling.

Even when your pup becomes an adult, do not forget to carry on with the training to reinforce what it has learnt. Your dog will be happy if you are happy, and you will be happy if your companion is obedient, loving and well-behaved.

Always keep your dog under full control.

useful *addresses*

UK Clubs, Societies and Associations

The Kennel Club (KC)
1 Clarges St
Piccadilly
London W1Y
General Enquiries 0171 493 6651
Registration Enquiries 0171 493 2001

The Agility Club,
Mr J Gilbert
100 Bedford Road
Barton-le-Clay
Beds MK45 4LS
Tel 01582 882366

Association of Pet Behavioural Counsellors (APBC)
257 Royal College Street
London NW1
Behavioural counsellors who act on veterinary referrals only.

Association of Pet Dog Trainers (APDT)
Peacocks Farm
Northchapel
Petworth
West Sussex GU28 9JB
Holds a list of Pet Dog Training Clubs that follow a code of ethics to promote kind methods of dog training.

Battersea Dogs Home
4 Battersea Park Rd
London SW8 4AA
Tel 0171 6223626

Blue Cross
Shilton Road
Burford
Oxon OX18 4PF
Tel 01993 822651
Provides a network of animal adoption centres, hospitals, a clinic and horse adoption scheme.

British Institute of Professional Dog Trainers (BIPDT)
General Secretary Tom Buckley
Bowstone Gate
Near Disley
Cheshire
Tel 016637 62772
Runs courses and gives certificates in dog training instruction, keeps list of registered and qualified instructors.

British Flyball Association (BFA)
Kevin McNicholas
50 Tudor Road
Barnet
Herts EN5 5NP
Tel 0181 449 7539

Canine Partners for Independence
Homewell House
22 Homewell
Havant
Hampshire PO9 1EE
Tel 01705 450156

useful *addresses*

Dogs for the Disabled
The Old Vicarage
London Road
Ryton-on-Dunsmore
Coventry
Warwickshire CV8 3ER
Tel 01203 302057

Federation of Pet Dog Trainers and Canine Behaviourists (FDTCB)
15 Lightbourne Avenue
Lytham St Annes
Lancashire FY8 1JE
Tel 01254 722923

Guide Dogs for the Blind
Hillfields
Burghfield
Reading
Berkshire
Tel 01734 835555.

Hearing Dogs for the Deaf
London Road
Lewknor
Oxfordshire
Tel 01844 353898.

International Sheepdog Society (ISDS)
Chesham House
47 Bromham Road
Bedford MK40 2AA
Tel 01234 352672

National Canine Defence League (NCDL)
19–26 Watley Street
Islington
London N1
Tel 0171 3880137
Network of rescue centres throughout Britain, with non-destruction policy.

National Dog Wardens Association (NDWA)
11 Raleigh Road
Wallisdown
Poole
Dorset BH12 5AL
Tel 01202 386657

People's Dispensary for Sick Animals (PDSA)
White Chapel Way
Priorslee
Telford
Shropshire TR2 9PG

PRO Dogs and PAT Dogs
Rocky Bank
4 New Rd
Ditton
Kent ME20 6AD
Tel 01732 848499
Works towards providing a better understanding of dogs and their benefits. Also operates Better British Breeder Scheme to put prospective owners in touch with good breeders.

Royal Society for the Prevention of Cruelty to Animals (RSPCA)
Causeway
Horsham
West Sussex
RH12 1HG
Tel 01403 64181

Support Dogs
PO Box 447
Sheffield S6 6YU
Tel 0114 2320026
Provides training for the disabled and their dogs.

U K Registry of Canine Behaviourists (UKRCB)
Mike Mullen
Dunsmore Kennels
London Road (A45)
Stretton-on-Dunsmore
Near Rugby
Warwickshire CV23 9HX
Tel 01203 542566

Waltham Centre, Pedigree Petfoods
Waltham on the Wolds
Melton Mowbray
Leics LE14 4RS

Wood Green Animal Shelter
London Road
Godmanchester
Huntingdon
Cambs PE18 8LJ
Tel 01480 830014

North American Clubs, Societies and Associations

The American Kennel Club (AKC)
51 Maddison Avenue
New York
NY 10010
USA

United Kennel Club
100 E. Kilgore Road
Kalamazoo
MI 49001–5598

Canadian Kennel Club
89 Skyway Avenue
Etobicoke
Ontario
Canada M9W 6R4

American Dog Owners Association
1654 Columbia Tpk.
Castleton
NY 12033

American Dog Trainers Network
161 West 4th Street
New York
NY 10014

Association of Pet Dog Trainers
PO Box 3734
Salinas
CA 93912

National Association of Dog Obedience Instructors
2286 East Steel Road
St Johns
MI 48879

North American Flyball Association
1342 Jeff Street
Ypsilanti
MI 48198

North American Working Dog Association, Inc.
Southeast Kreisgruppe
PO Box 833
Brunswick
GA 31521

Therapy Dogs International
1536 Morris Place
Hillside
NJ 07205

Magazines and Newspapers

Obedience Competitor Magazine
PO Box 1044
Haxey
Doncaster DN9 2JL
Tel 01427 753918
Fax 01427 754035
Available by subscription, or at major obedience shows. Covers obedience events, reports, show adverts, training tips, and news affecting and from the world of Competitive Obedience.

Front and Finish
PO Box 333
Galesburg
IL 61402–0333
USA
American newspaper on dog training and related issues.

Off Lead
Arner Publications
13 Clinton St
Clark Mills
New York NY1332
USA
American magazine publication on dog training.

The Author

Angela White
PO Box 1044
Haxey
Doncaster DN9 2JL
Tel 01427 753918
Fax 01427 754035

useful
reading

by the same author

Everybody Can Train Their Own Dog
A unique A–Z reference guide to training your dog. Whether you are a seasoned pet owner, dog show enthusiast, professional handler or instructor, or completely new to dogs, problem-solving, training techniques, behavioural understanding and much more is packed into this easy-to-read handbook with full-colour photographs throughout its 255 pages. Published by TFH Inc and available from TFH Publications (address on facing page). ISBN 0-86622-524-2

Happy Dogs... Happy Winners!
The Complete Competitive Obedience Training Manual.
Sound, constructive advice on how to enjoy training while gaining the best from your dog, whatever its type or character. Step-by-step techniques, easy to read and follow. Kind motivational methods. Fun training with winning in mind.
Published by Rainbow Publishing, PO Box 1044, Haxey, Doncaster.DN9 2JL.
Tel 01427 753918 Fax 01427 754035
ISBN 1-899057-00-5

other useful reading

Appleby, Pauline, **How to Work with Dogs** (How to Books)

Bailey, Joan, **How to Help Gundogs Train Themselves** (Swan Valley Press)

Benjamin, Carol Lea, **Surviving Your Dog's Adolescence** (Howell Books)

Benjamin, Carol Lea, **Dog Tricks** (Howell Books)

Carruthers, Barrie and Bing, Keith, **Love Me, Love My Dog** (TFH)

De Prisco, Andrew and Johnson, James B. **Mini Atlas of Dog Breeds** (TFH)

De Prisco, Andrew and Johnson, James B. **Canine Lexicon** (TFH)

Dunbar, Dr Ian, **Dog Behaviour** (TFH)

useful reading

Fogle, Bruce, **The Dog's Mind** (Pelham Books)

Jackson, Frank, **Dictionary of Canine Terms** (Crowood)

Johnston, Bruce, **Harnessing Thought** (Lennard Associates)

Lane, D.R., and Cooper, B. (eds) **Veterinary Nursing** (Pergamon)

Lewis, Peter, **Teaching Dog Agility** (Canine Publications)

Pryor, Karen, **Don't Shoot The Dog** (Bantam Books)

Pryor, Karen, **A Dog and a Dolphin** (Sunshine Books)

Pryor, Karen, **On Behaviour** (Sunshine Books)

Walker, Stephen, **Animal Learning** (Routledge & Kegan Paul)

Wilcox, Bonnie and Walkowicz, Chris, **Atlas of Dog Breeds** (TFH)

Wilks, Gary, **A Behaviour Sampler** (Sunshine Books)

index